To
Martha Sue
great to meet
at NHS
Wendy
Jordan
9/17/19

PRAISE FOR JORDAN GOLDRICH AND *WORKPLACE WARRIOR*

"Jordan Goldrich provides a unique perspective on executives who get labeled as abrasive or as bullies. He recognizes that demeaning, bullying behavior is not acceptable and that hard-driving, results-focused personalities are needed in our complex, rapidly changing business environment. Thus, he challenges hard-driving executives to express their warrior spirit while minimizing unintended negative impact."

—MARSHALL GOLDSMITH, #1 *New York Times* best-selling author of *Triggers, MOJO,* and *What Got You Here Won't Get You There*

"Jordan Goldrich applies his own insights about his experience as a workplace warrior to help other no-bullshit executives achieve their objectives without alienating coworkers. Written to help these leaders elevate their warrior styles to higher levels of success, the book offers specific steps to increase their interpersonal effectiveness in the workplace."

—LAURA CRAWSHAW, Ph.D., BCC, President, Executive Insight Development Group, Inc.

"Jordan is the quintessential no bull-shit corporate executive coach. I could not think of a better fit for an advisor to work with and coach the C-suite executive and leaders who are identified as "workplace warriors"—aka abrasive/aggressive leader and/or bully. Jordan presents undoubtedly a unique concept in identifying this archetype as a warrior who we typically associate as heroes. Jordan presents that these individuals bring a unique perspective in the workplace and society. He challenges us to recognize these unique characteristics and open the doors of acceptability while challenging the "warrior" to funnel these traits through more acceptable channels . . . "

—**CB BOWMAN,** MBA, MCEC, BCC, CMC, CEO & Founder of
the Association of Corporate Executive Coaches (ACEC);
MEECO Leadership Institute

"Workplace Warrior is a necessary guide for leaders who are invaluable to their organizations—*AND*—who are in need of a few modifications to their mindsets and behavior. What makes this book so powerful is the way it presents the journey for leaders in a way that does not diminish their unique and highly valued skills. Yet the book also provides just the right shifts these leaders need to make to attract more people to willingly follow them."

—**FRANK WAGNER,** Practice Leader, Marshall Goldsmith's
Stakeholder Centered Coaching

"While other thought leaders are trying to change hard-driving, high-achieving executives beyond recognition, Jordan Goldrich has figured out how to harness their power to carry them and their teams to greater success."

—WILLIAM W. EIGNER, Partner, Procopio

"*Workplace Warrior* is a must-read for all current and aspiring leaders. The world needs leaders who are not afraid to hold people accountable for their actions and, at the same time, have the ability to be compassionate. People are often afraid to be labeled a "No-Bullshit Leader." Jordan addresses this issue head on and brings the conversation to the surface. His examples will be invaluable when you think you need support and need to know you are not alone. After all, who wants to be shoveling "bullshit" all day long?"

—CINDY ZURCHIN, ED.D, Co-Author,
The Whale Done! School, Motivational Speaker,
Trainer, Business Consultant, and Coach

WORKPLACE

WARRIOR

PEOPLE SKILLS

for the

NO-BULLSHIT
EXECUTIVE

WORKPLACE
WARRIOR

JORDAN GOLDRICH

with **WALTER G. MEYER**

GREENLEAF
BOOK GROUP PRESS

Published by Greenleaf Book Group Press
Austin, Texas
www.gbgpress.com

Distributed by Greenleaf Book Group

For ordering information or special discounts for bulk purchases, please contact Greenleaf Book Group at PO Box 91869, Austin, TX 78709, 512.891.6100.

Design and composition by Greenleaf Book Group
Cover design by Greenleaf Book Group
Image Copyright TRONIN ANDREI. Used under license from Shutterstock.com

For permission to reproduce copyrighted material, grateful acknowledgment is made to the following sources:
From *Smarter Faster Better: The Transformative Power of Real Productivity* by Charles Duhigg. (For excerpt from "What Google Learned From Its Quest to Build the Perfect Team" as it appeared in *The New York Times Magazine*.) Copyright © 2016 by Charles Duhigg. Reproduced by permission of the author.
From "Google Spent 2 Years Studying 180 Teams. The Most Successful Ones Shared These 5 Traits" by Michael Schneider, from *Inc.* magazine, July 19, 2017. Copyright © by Michael Schneider. Reproduced by permission of Mansueto Ventures LLC.
From "4 Reasons Why You Need a Personal Mission Statement" by Rhett Power, from *Inc.* magazine, February 19, 2016. Copyright © 2016 by Rhett Power. Reproduced by permission of Mansueto Ventures LLC.
For two photographs of chickens. Copyright © by William M. Muir. Reproduced by permission of William M. Muir. All rights reserved.
Credits continued on page 198, which serves as an extension of the copyright page.

Publisher's Cataloging-in-Publication data is available.

Print ISBN: 978-1-62634-651-2

eBook ISBN: 978-1-62634-652-9

Part of the Tree Neutral® program, which offsets the number of trees consumed in the production and printing of this book by taking proactive steps, such as planting trees in direct proportion to the number of trees used: www.treeneutral.com

Printed in the United States of America on acid-free paper

19 20 21 22 23 24   10 9 8 7 6 5 4 3 2 1

First Edition

CONTENTS

APPENDICES

Foreword

Jordan Goldrich's *Workplace Warrior* explores the values that enable us to achieve our missions. It gives us the means to be successful and satisfied. It shows us how to make a difference. His book fully acknowledges that sometimes our behavior in service of our values may be upsetting to other people. But he offers remedies that can help us get the job done while we learn how to maintain good and productive relationships with our co-workers. Jordan does this by shedding light on the warrior spirit. His honoring of this tradition is long overdue. We will all benefit from it.

I have known Jordan for many years and witnessed his personal learning curve grow out of his direct experience helping transitioning Navy SEALs and other members of our special operations community. He was able to develop keen insights into the challenges these heroes face as they transferred their mindset and skills to the challenges of pursuing success in civilian life. Jordan recognized that many of the special operations forces' values that help achieve excellence may also at times show up as behavior that is experienced as abrasive or alienating. As a result, Jordan shows us that practicing the complete set of warrior values will allow us to take our effectiveness to an even higher level, while avoiding creating a negative impact. He provides the skills and perspectives to make that happen. He shows us that we can be strong without being bullies.

In late 1999, I joined the Center for Creative Leadership (CCL) as a manager in assessing and coaching operations. I soon realized that my style of getting things done was a poor fit for the new culture. My leadership and managerial behavior had been honed in small and midsize businesses in fast-paced, entrepreneurial, and for-profit settings. Now I was in an academic, non-profit, research-based, tradition-rich, training and development organization steadily operating with a different culture and tempo.

To be sure, I had always known I had flaws. I had worked on them off and on. And, they had only slightly shaded my success in previous ventures. But these same flaws suddenly became career derailers in a very different culture. Don't get me wrong: I'm not criticizing the CCL culture. I am only saying it was a poor fit for me. Think of putting a salt-water fish in a fresh-water lake.

CCL has done years of credible research identifying what behavioral tendencies can stall a career. Five major derailers have been identified and validated—and I fell into the grips of some of them. Under pressure and frustration, I became abrasive often enough to build a bad local reputation. Sometimes I became impatient, judgmental, or critical. And organizations remember those moments.

A signature contribution to the field was the Center's SBI feedback model, that Jordan discusses in the book. Thankfully, I received feedback in reaction to the things I said and the way I said them. I didn't like being the kind of person I was hearing about. I knew that every bit of the feedback that was given to me was done so with the best of intentions. And so, I took it to heart. I identified some behavior change goals. I accessed the rich leadership development resources available to me at the Center. I took assessments, reviewed publications, consulted fellow experts, and reached out for collegial support. I learned about spanning the boundaries between myself and people who thought and functioned differently. I learned new leadership and communication styles. All of this enabled me to diversify my actions in order to be more effective with people who were singing in different keys.

But it was a hard journey filled with frustration and self-criticism, and fueled by the drumbeat of what I heard: "Don't be so direct and harsh" instead of what I wanted to hear: "Thanks for caring enough to get things done around here." No one expressed appreciation for the warrior in me while I was trying to contain my abrasive impulses.

The valuable advice Jordan offers in this book provides what I would consider to be a fairly complete profile of what I have learned about leadership and management—the hard way—over the course of a diverse career. I discovered that type of learning to be the most challenging (and also the most valuable) when I found myself in the right position for my skill set—but in the wrong culture for my temperament.

Jordan gets it. He understands that the best warriors on the planet are both strong and humane. He also understands the challenge leaders face in a time when many people enable and exploit the "poor me" hypersensitivity of self-perceived "victims." Some of these people may become upset by any kind of feedback, direction, or disappointment and take shelter by crying foul cloaked in social justice grievances. But Jordan's advice is as applicable for dealing with people who play these games as it is for dealing with people who simply have a legitimate dislike for being treated harshly. Jordan's book empowers the warrior in all of us with greater humanity, because he understands that the current reaction to warrior behavior in Western culture has become polarized and unappreciated.

Jordan understands that the strengths of the warrior and the warrior mindset must be honored even as we strive to sand off the splinters that may alienate some people. He shows us how to honor the warrior spirit and soften the roughness without compromising the warrior mission.

Go out and be the best warriors on the planet.

E. Wayne Hart,
PhD Senior Fellow
Center for Creative Leadership
March 16, 2019

ACKNOWLEDGMENTS

I want to thank my co-author, Walter G. Meyer, for his many contributions to *Workplace Warrior*. As the author of the critically-acclaimed novel *Rounding Third*, the widely-produced stage play *GAM3RS*, the co-author of four other books and hundreds of newspaper and magazine articles, Walter readily shares his industry expertise with other authors about the book-writing process. Walter has a deep knowledge of the research and cultural issues addressed in *Workplace Warrior*, and he challenged to me to consider important alternative perspectives.

I would also like to thank my Greenleaf Book Group team—Sally Garland, Jen Glynn, Neil Gonzalez, Olivia McCoy, Kristine Peyre-Ferry, Daniel Sandoval, and Nathan True. They were all highly knowledgeable and supportive throughout the process.

I have had the honor of volunteering as an executive coach for

The Honor Foundation (THF), a non-profit organization dedicated to helping the US special operations community transition to civilian life. This volunteering was an opportunity for me to serve my country and the men and women protecting it. When I began working with THF about two years ago, I believed I was within months of publishing this book. But as I came to understand their concepts about what it means to be a warrior, about tribe, and about leading elite teams, I realized I was going to need to rewrite what I had written. I want to acknowledge THF for making me see what my book was missing. I continue to receive a lot more from this organization than I give, and I encourage you all to explore becoming associated with an incredible group of outstanding human beings.

THF founder and former CEO, Joe Musselman, has extraordinary vision and leadership. In addition to contributing to my understanding of leadership, Joe introduced me to the organizations of General Stanley McChrystal and Simon Sinek, and he facilitated the process of receiving permission to include their important perspectives. Joe has recently become a board member of The Honor For Life Foundation, whose goal it is to create a $100-million endowment to benefit the mission of The Honor Foundation in perpetuity.

Joe Lara, THF Senior Director of Operations in San Diego, reviewed my understanding of the Navy SEALs' ethos and other special operations personnel. His input was invaluable, and I continue to learn from him. I had the opportunity to observe Jeff Pottinger, THF Vice President of Programs, facilitate a workshop based on Simon Sinek's *Find Your Why* for the special operations fellows attending the program. He graciously offered to coach me on taking my own *why* statement to a more powerful level. As VP, Chief of People Operations, Phil Dana provided a very powerful orientation to THF and to the "tribe" of our special operations forces. THF executive coach Miguel de Jesus strongly suggested that I write the appendix "How to Select an Executive Coach." I am grateful, and the advice was much appreciated.

A number of my colleagues and friends made valuable contributions by sharing their deep knowledge and expertise. I want to recognize and thank them.

Wayne Hart wrote the foreword, reviewed several chapters, and helped me adapt material from his book, *Feedback in Performance Reviews*, for chapter 14, "Speaking Powerfully without Damaging Relationships." He assisted me in obtaining permission from the Center for Creative Leadership (CCL), who is the publisher. Wayne is a Senior Fellow with CCL, one of the most recognized organizations providing leadership development and executive coaching in the world.

Robert McClure introduced me to the Stanford University Compassion Cultivation Training. He reviewed the material in chapter 6 on neuroscience and the material in chapter 7, "Making the Commitment to Cultivate Compassion for People Your Brain Tells You Don't Deserve It." Bob also helped me obtain permission to quote the intellectual property developed by Stanford and now licensed to the Compassion Institute, LLC. If you are interested in Compassion Cultivation Training, I encourage you to contact them.

Laura Crawshaw reviewed several chapters and gave me permission to reprint her self-test "Are You Abrasive" as well as other excerpts from her book, *Taming the Abrasive Manager: How to End Unnecessary Roughness in the Workplace*. Laura is the founder of *The Boss Whispering Institute* which trains coaches in the only defined method to date for coaching abrasive leaders. I encourage you to contact the Institute to locate an executive coach with this exceptional training.

Don Sloane, Director of the Center for Cognitive Behavioral

Therapy in St. Louis, introduced me to Tai Chi and was a mentor in developing my understanding of Eastern philosophies. He is referenced in chapter 6 in the section on martial arts. I encourage you to look for his book, *Six Pathways to Happiness: Mindfulness and Psychology in Chinese Buddhism*, if you are interested in Buddhist philosophy.

Kerry Delk and Andrew Chirchirillo are highly respected psychologists with deep expertise in assessment and diagnosis. Both contributed valuable input to chapter 2, "Types of No-Bullshit Executives and What Drives Them." Kerry founded the Newport Psychology Group in Newport Beach, CA, and Andrew is both a clinical psychologist and psychoanalyst, who founded the Clayton Clinical Group in St. Louis Missouri.

Frank Wagner is a Founding Member of The Marshall Goldsmith Group and oversees the Stakeholder Centered Coaching certification process for Marshall Goldsmith. He reviewed my understanding of feedforward discussed in chapter 10, "Conduct Your Research."

Pamela Richarde reviewed my appendix "How to Select an Executive Coach." Pamela is the Managing Director and Executive Coach with InnerVision Enterprises LLC. She is a former president of the International Coach Federation.

Fran Fisher is a Master Certified Coach and President of FJ Fisher Coaching and Consulting. As mentioned in chapter 9, "Tell People Who You Are and What You Stand For," Fran's program, "Living Your Vision™," provided me with the foundation for identifying my core purpose.

I received important support, perspective, and expertise from my authors' mastermind group: Gregg Ward, Cynthia Burnham, Walter Meyer, and Chris Witt were all published authors and successful consultants when I joined. In addition to sharing their knowledge and expertise on writing and publishing a book, they gave me valuable input on my tendency to be abrasive.

I would not be the coach that I am today, without my 12+ years of work with the Center for Creative Leadership (CCL). In particular, I want to acknowledge Rich Been, Rosa Belzer, Wayne Hart, Kevin O'Gorman, David Powell, Doug Riddle, and Sheryl White.

I want to recognize my partners in CUSTOMatrix, Inc. I wouldn't be the executive coach I am today without the perspective of Eric Chriss, who is the founder and CEO. Eric is one of the few chief financial officers I know who understands that "everything is connected" and that consultants and executive coaches need to "deliver everything." Eric was crucial in helping me develop into a trusted advisor. I also learned a great deal from my partners, Tom Erickson and Robin Stephenson. Tom shared his deep experience as a vice president of human resources who has been part of executive teams that have managed thirteen mergers and acquisitions. He is an excellent executive coach and a great support. Robin contributed her expertise as an entrepreneur who has owned several successful businesses. She has trained women leaders and support staff in seven countries and has served on the board of directors for three national organizations.

The Association of Corporate Executive Coaches (ACEC) and its partner organization, the MEECO Leadership Institute, provided me with the opportunity to learn from and "hang out with" the top executive coaches and experts on employment science. CB Bowman is the CEO and founder of both organizations, which define master level corporate executive coaches as "enterprise-wide business partners™" who must have, among other assets, both leadership and business experience as part of their coaching portfolio. I am honored to have been able to learn from CB and other top-level members.

I want to mention three important teachers. Rick Kinyon, mentioned in chapter 8, was my first leadership mentor. Nick Krnich was the owner of the company we built and sold to WellPoint Health Networks, a Fortune 500 company. Louis Spain, mentioned in chapter 4, taught me what is now known as lean and six sigma.

I would like to thank my family for all they have contributed in terms of support and facing the challenges required to build character. My parents, Howard and Renee Goldrich, are the loud New York family I describe in chapter 1. My uncle and aunt, Seymour and Marion Furman, were not quite as loud unless they were around my parents. All were highly educated and deeply passionate people who taught me about integrity, accountability, and what it means to be competent. They also helped me realize that those of us who are experienced by others as abrasive are nevertheless valued members of our diverse communities. Because I am an only child, my cousins Michael and Stuart Furman and Leslie Basiago are like siblings. Stuart's wife Jayne has been a member of the family for many years and Michael's partner Dea Bell is now a member of the family as well. Together we have experienced the joy and craziness of being a family.

My wife, Deborah Moser, is my loving partner and my greatest support. She has shared her knowledge and expertise as both a leader and a master trainer. She is a warrior who—to paraphrase the Navy SEALs' ethos—has integrity, loyalty, and honor. She is never out of the fight. Together we have come to understand that you have a choice to be alone or to be with a strong, independent person whom you love and respect. If you choose the second, you will not be alone. However, you will frequently be annoyed for the rest of your life. I love it when she tells me she does not want to be annoyed by anyone but me.

Thank you all for your contributions and your support.

THE BATTLE PLAN

A no-bullshit executive demonstrates the ability to get results in seemingly impossible situations. They accomplish this with a work ethic that accepts nothing less than always giving their all and making sure their projects are done on time and within budget. They are always goal focused. They drive for results, demand discipline, and hold their people and everyone else accountable—relentlessly. Even above-average performers may wonder where the no-bullshit executive gets the energy to keep going.

Warriors are the elite class of no-bullshit executives—the best of the best. This elite group includes military leaders—literal warriors—committed to completing their mission and protecting both their team and noncombatants in situations most people would describe as impossible. As used in this book, the term includes business leaders working around the clock to launch a start-up or bring a failing business back to profitability. Warriors can be leaders of nonprofit organizations working tirelessly to serve under-resourced communities. They are doctors and nurses in an emergency room dedicated to saving injured people after a severe accident. Mothers and fathers can be warriors as well. This book is intended to help you embrace that elite status and to use it to accomplish incredible things.

So, as a no-bullshit executive—and maybe a warrior—what is your motivation? If you are like most no-bullshit executives, you have a combination of three motives: being the best and/or being right, achieving great results, and serving. Each of us has our own unique mix of these qualities, but they're the crucial makeup of a no-bullshit executive. Your motivation to be the best makes you want to become CEO, destroy your competitors, and generally kick butt. As you have evolved, you have grown from wanting to win for yourself to wanting your team or your company to be number one.

Your motivation to achieve makes you commit to accomplishing great—some people would say *impossible*—things. For you, it might be turning around a failing company, achieving unbelievable business results, or designing a disruptive innovation. If you are in the medical field, that goal might be curing a disease that takes millions of lives and, until now, has been incurable.

Your motivation to serve makes you commit to eradicating poverty, ending oppression, or helping disabled veterans. On the lighter side, it may make you want to make technology easier to use or more available or to make legal or financial information available at a much lower cost. It may also make you committed to understanding and meeting the needs of your work colleagues and reports.

However, your high standards and constant drive for success might leave you frustrated and annoyed when others do not live up to your standards. Sometimes, you are not appreciated for your contribution to the success of your company or organization. You may have been called names like *bully, jerk, hyena, narcissist,* or *toxic.* If you are female, these names might have included *bitch* or *ballbuster.* In our current employee-relations environment, you are vulnerable to complaints and job action for disrespect, breach of company policy, discrimination, and creating a hostile work environment. Like many no-bullshit executives, you may think this is a bunch of politically correct garbage.

In some cases, you feel you have simply given honest, matter-of-fact feedback, and the people who received it were oversensitive. In other cases, you must admit you were impatient or sarcastic or perhaps crossed the line to disrespect. Still, it is hard for you to understand how it is possible that this is more of an issue than the behavior and performance of people who are not as committed as you, not as honest as you, and not producing as much as you.

You have some theories. Many no-bullshit executives think they get unfairly criticized because America has become "soft." They ask themselves and others, "How is it bad that I expect people to perform at a consistently high level? Is it unreasonable to expect the people I work with to be able to deal with being told their performance is not what it could or should be? Isn't that just treating them like adults? Are people so damn sensitive that they can't handle an honest conversation?"

I get exasperated when I hear that some schools will not let children play tag in school because being "it" might hurt their self-esteem. In 2015, James Harrison, then of the Pittsburgh Steelers, set off a national debate when he refused to let his children keep participation trophies they had received in school. He wrote on Instagram,

> "I came home to find out that my boys received two trophies for nothing, participation trophies! While I am very proud of my boys for everything they do and will encourage them till the day I die, these trophies will be given back until they *earn* a real trophy. I'm sorry I'm not sorry for believing that everything in life should be earned and I'm not about to raise two boys to be men by making them believe that they are entitled to something just because they tried their best . . . cause sometimes your best is not enough, and that should drive you to want to do better . . . not cry and whine until somebody gives you something to shut you up and keep you happy."

I see situations like this and can sympathize with Mr. Harrison's impatience with our overprotective, even coddling culture. The purpose of this book is to help you continue to drive for success while covering your butt in our current, politically correct (or just overprotective) environment. On your way, I'll be advising you to do *the least you can do*. You'll see what I mean.

THE LEAST YOU CAN DO

"The Least You Can Do," has two meanings: Either may apply to you.

The first meaning is literal. You may believe that the pressure to be more respectful, to go easier on coworkers, or to get along better with others is a lot of PC nonsense. At the same time, you recognize that the recent events in the corporate world, Hollywood, and politics mean that if you continue leading and communicating in the same way, you risk an unhappy or shortened career. You are faced with the dilemma of protecting yourself by changing, although you do not believe you should have to make these changes. In this case, you may only want to literally do the very least you would have to do to protect yourself.

The second meaning is the pursuit of the morally, ethically, or professionally "right" thing to do. These are actions you would do even if all the pressure disappeared and you received no reward. For example, if someone in a wheelchair asked for help, you would certainly assist them to cross the street. If they offered to pay you, you might say, "Absolutely, not. This was the least I could do."

If I do my job, you will decide to adopt the mindset and people skills presented in this book because they are *the least you can do* in this second sense. The good news is that, if you adopt this attitude and these tools, you can be 100% authentic, and you will be even more successful in achieving your goals than you already are. At the same time, you will be seen as tougher than you were seen before.

You might ask, "How can I hold my reports and others accountable and not be accused of abrasive or bullying behavior?" Picture, if you will, talking to a friend in a park; let's call him *Jim*. You notice that Jim is absentmindedly stepping backward, and you notice that there is a cliff behind him. He's getting closer to the edge with each backward step.

One possibility would be to interrupt and say, "Jim, stop stepping backward, you idiot. There's a cliff behind you. Why don't you look where you are going?" Obviously, this is done with a critical tone, even reprimanding.

A second possibility would be to interrupt and say, "Jim, if you keep stepping backward, you may fall off the cliff." This would be done using an urgent, direct tone with the intention of alerting Jim to take action to avoid hurting himself.

Either way, you should say something, right? It's the least you can do. Telling reports that unacceptable behavior is unacceptable is a crucial part of leadership. If their performance will lead to reduced annual pay raises, bonuses, or perhaps discipline and termination, shouldn't they know before that process is irreversible? If they are backing toward a metaphorical cliff, shouldn't you warn them of the danger?

The second example is similar to the first, but with a shift in intention and, therefore, in tone. If you do this with the good-faith intention to alert them to what they need to do, you avoid the unintended negative impact of speaking in a way they experience as demeaning. The impact is even greater, because when you express it in a manner that expresses concern and respect for them as a person, they cannot dismiss you as an asshole.

What makes this book different is the perspective about what it means to be a no-bullshit executive—and a warrior—that I have come to understand as a result of my volunteer work with The Honor Foundation (THF). THF is a nonprofit organization that helps the US Special Operations Forces transition to civilian life. These include the Navy SEALs, the Marine Raiders, the Green Berets, and the Air Force Pararescuemen and Combat Controllers.

Because of my work with THF, I am better able to articulate that your warrior spirit is not recognized and appreciated in our current culture. Ultimately, this book is about challenging you to become a better no-bullshit executive. The point is not to convince you to start taking bullshit. It's to help you become a better warrior.

NO-BULLSHIT EXECUTIVES' DRIVERS AND TYPES

CHAPTER 1

How I Got Smacked in the Head and Decided to Do the Least I Can Do

The phone rang, and I heard my boss's voice.

"Jordan, can you come to my office?"

I walked down the hall, knocked, and went in. There, sitting with my boss was the vice president of human resources, whose office was a three-hour drive from ours.

Being a quick study, I thought, *This is not good.*

My boss proceeded to tell me she was terminating my employment for mismanaging my budget. I was confused, because I had been raising questions about the size of the overhead number corporate finance had included in my budget. I knew something was wrong, and I had requested information to determine what it was. I never got the information.

The human resources VP, like any competent HR professional, said something like, "We are not going to discuss this today; the decision has been made."

I was walked out the door. It was the first time I had ever been fired. I was in shock.

A week passed, and I was in a local bagel shop, where I happened to run into the consultant from the finance unit who had been working with me.

"Jordan, I owe you an apology."

"Why?" I asked.

"Do you remember the conversations where you told me that something was wrong with your overhead and I looked at you as if I didn't know what you were talking about?"

"Yes."

"And do you remember requesting a breakdown of your overhead, but I never gave it to you?"

"Yes."

"Well, I did know what you were talking about, but I was told by our boss that I would lose my job if I told you or gave you the breakdown."

I was surprised but not stunned. I hadn't had a good relationship with my boss for a long time. I had seen her to be indirect—if not dishonest—before, and while I respected her expertise, I didn't respect what I perceived was her lack of integrity.

I went outside and sat in my car to take in what I had just heard. It was about 90 degrees. I was sweating, and my mind was racing. I began to think about how this had come about. I believed I had clear evidence that I had been set up. Who would deny that I had a right to feel angry and victimized? I experienced a combination of rage and disbelief.

Man, she got me, I thought.

But I dislike feeling bitter and victimized—a lot—so I said to myself, "OK, big shot. See if you can actually apply the viewpoint you have communicated with others over the years." As a therapist and consultant, I had suggested that if you need other people to change in order to feel good about yourself, that is the path to disappointment, bitterness, and victimization. Success and fulfillment is based on focusing on what you can control.

I began my self-examination, using the words of wisdom in Viktor Frankl's book *Man's Search for Meaning*. Dr. Frankl was a Jewish psychiatrist who had been in a concentration camp. His book is about the kinds of reactions and survival strategies he observed in himself and in others. He said several things that have had immense meaning to me regarding how to face adversity:

- "He who has a *why* to live for can bear with almost any *how*." (Quote is from Nietzsche.)

- "It is not freedom from conditions, but it is freedom to take a stand toward the conditions."

- "*[It does] not really matter what we expected from life, but rather what life expected from us.* We [need] to stop asking about the meaning of life, and instead to think of ourselves as those who were being questioned by life—daily and hourly."
- "When we are no longer able to change a situation—just think of an incurable disease such as inoperable cancer—we are challenged to change ourselves."

I had to admit that while I had been "got" by my boss in a dishonest way, I was not in a concentration camp, so I had much to be grateful for. I was certainly concerned about the impact on my wife and on my family's finances. I knew I would face many challenges, but none would be life threatening. I did not want to let myself sink into a pit of anger and bitterness.

So I decided to take Dr. Frankl's words of wisdom to heart and choose another path. I started by thinking about the mindset I offer to my clients when they have been subjected to unfair treatment or experienced painful circumstances.

Dr. Frankl said that one of the keys to coming through adversity is having a purpose. Simon Sinek and others now refer to this as having a *why*. I knew that my *why* had something to do with making a positive impact on the world, but I had not fully articulated it. I had been too busy taking care of making myself successful.

I started by considering what life might be asking of me. I asked myself the questions I used with my counseling and consulting clients who experienced mistreatment and misfortune:

- What did I control in this situation?

- Is there anything I could have done to achieve a different outcome?

Regarding the question, "What did I control?" I had to admit that I hadn't respected my boss's integrity for quite a while and that I had let this show. I had not used profanity or disrespectful language. Nor had I been insubordinate. But I certainly had challenged what I saw as problems in her plans of action, both privately and in meetings. And there were certainly times when my tone was critical.

Throughout our professional relationship, I knew that she wanted more deference than I was giving her. I had felt justified in my way of relating to her because of what I saw as gaps in her integrity. After all, why should I have to worry about my attitude and tone with someone who does not deserve it?

I also had to admit that, throughout my life and career, supervisors, coaches, and friends had warned me that I needed to be less opinionated and more respectful, that I needed to be more willing to be part of the team. One of my early mentors once told me, "Shut up when other people don't want to hear what you think is your obviously correct point of view."

During these conversations, I had often thought, "I can't believe that people are upset about my tone and not about the fact that this person is not doing their job or not thinking clearly." And, to be truthful, I did not see how I would have the energy to constantly manage my tone *and* work my tail off. After all, I was getting results. Wasn't that what mattered most? Wasn't the requirement that I dance around the truth with people who were not thinking clearly, not performing, or acting without integrity just a bunch of politically correct bullshit?

5

So, on that 90-degree summer day, it hit me that if I did not want to feel victimized and miserable for the next 10 years, I needed to treat this situation as if I were being smacked in the head by a two-by-four with the message *Cut it out.*

I made a commitment to close the valve on my internal pressure cooker that had allowed me to rationalize being impatient, frustrated, and sarcastic with others when the stress got high. It was the commitment that I was missing. When I simply removed the permission I had given myself to be abrasive, I was able to significantly lower the amount of frustration and impatience in my words and tone.

Don't get me wrong. My friends and colleagues I have met in recent years still think I can be overly direct and sometimes tactless. But people who knew me 20 years ago think I have become a different person.

Let me give you some background on how I got here.

I grew up in a family that was loud, even by New York standards. I remember being 11 years old and going to my apartment on the ninth floor with my friend after playing stickball in the playground.

As we got off the elevator, he said, "I don't think we should go in."

"Why?" I said.

"Because your parents are fighting."

I paused to listen to their loud, impatient tone and exasperated, even disrespectful words and said, "They're not fighting. They're talking to each other."

It was simply the way I learned to communicate.

My family expressed itself in many ways that, as I learned later, would result in negative reactions in most cultures within the United

States and the rest of the world. For some reason, it took me a long time to understand this.

When I was 12 years old, I decided it was time to express my political opinion at a family gathering. After I did, my psychiatrist uncle, Seymour, said, "Jordan, you're a moron." Now, I did not think for one second that Seymour thought I was a moron. I knew he loved and respected me. This was my family's typical way of saying *You haven't thought this through*.

(Today, the word *moron* has become an offensive and unacceptable term to refer to people with intellectual disabilities. I guarantee you that my family did not intend this meaning. I have chosen not to change it here, because I want to give you a true sense of my family culture and the kinds of communication that got wired into my brain. I recognize the sensitivity of using this term and hope that no one is offended.)

So, over the years, my brain became programmed to trigger disrespectful things I should say during discussions, debates, and arguments. It is not easy to change long-term habits that are wired into your brain's neural pathways.

Although our tone and language seemed disrespectful, my family believed that all people should be respected. I recognize that this is counterintuitive, but it was true.

I grew up in a city housing project that provided partial rent subsidies for returning World War II veterans. (Although he was a podiatrist, my father was not a successful businessman.) Everyone I knew was working class. The project had people of many nationalities, races, and religions. I was taught to focus on a person's character and not their religion or background, the color of their skin, their sexual orientation, or anything else.

My family culture involved what New York working people might call *straight talk*. When someone said something you thought was stupid, you told them directly that it was stupid. The style was wired into my brain through years of practice. According to current research, there may be a genetic factor as well.

Sitting that day in my car in the 90-degree heat, I realized that my style of communication was not consistent with my core value of respect for all people. I made the commitment that, going forward, I would communicate with compassion and respect for the human being in front of me, regardless of how much I disagreed with their thinking or behavior. Today, I refer to this as *making the commitment to cultivate compassion for people my brain is telling me do not deserve it.*

Many of the driven, results-oriented executives I have worked with or coached are religious people who believe their job on Earth is to do God's will. From St. Augustine to Mahatma Gandhi and the Dalai Lama, philosophers and prophets have said some version of "love the sinner but hate the sin."

What I have discovered is that when I am successful at fulfilling my commitment to be compassionate and respectful regardless of what the other person is doing or saying, I am actually more influential and more powerful than when I am undisciplined enough to follow the preprogrammed suggestions my brain makes about what I should say.

Treating people with respect does not mean letting them off the hook. The executives I coach who are not identified as abrasive are often uncomfortable giving negative feedback. I often hear something like, "I am not ready to be that direct. I don't want to discourage them." My experience is that when you tell people that their performance or behavior does not meet expectations sooner rather than later, they are more likely to understand and act on that understanding. When you clearly describe the negative impact of their performance or behavior in a respectful manner, they are more likely to authentically change. You make it less likely that they will be able to rationalize away your message by telling themselves you are a jerk.

If you are, in fact, abrasive rather than tough, then, like me, you are creating unintended negative consequences for yourself and others. The good news is you do not have to remake your personality. In fact, your drive, your focus on results, and your no-bullshit attitude are tremendously valuable to your organizations, your coworkers, your friends, and your family.

CHAPTER 2

Types of No-Bullshit Executives and What Drives Them

Prior to identifying the four types of no-bullshit executives, it will be helpful to discuss the motivations that drive their communication style and behavior that others may identify as abrasive. I want to be clear that these types of no-bullshit executives and their underlying motivations are based on my observations about myself, my observations from working with executives, combined with my reading of applicable literature and my experience as a licensed clinical social worker.

THERE IS A PURPOSE

Most no-bullshit executives are committed to and motivated by being the best and/or being right, achieving great results, and serving others, regardless of how long or arduous the mission or project. Being the best can either mean extremely competitive (as in the highest position or the highest salary) or being masterful.

Even high performers wonder where these executives get the energy. People who are not as committed to being the best and/or being right, achieving great results, or serving others may experience these executives' expectations as unreasonable, abrasive, or abusive, even when an objective third party would agree the executive has been appropriate and respectful. And, of course, these executives may also cross the line into communicating with an abrasive or bullying style.

THERE CAN BE A CULTURAL
COMPONENT TO ABRASIVENESS

In my experience, many executives who are identified as abrasive were raised in cultures or families in which loud, direct, challenging communication is normal. Their friends and families may not consider their behavior to be abrasive. In fact, their families may consider them to be caring people and may accept what others see as abrasiveness as normal communication. At worst, they may consider it human imperfection. This was certainly the case with my family. Speaking softly and carefully was interpreted as not being confident or as being cold, uncaring, or manipulative.

THE BEHAVIOR IS OFTEN A DEFENSIVE RESPONSE

Most no-bullshit executives experience less than great performance from others as a personal threat or attack. Their responses to that threat or attack may then be identified by the recipients or observers as abrasive or bullying. Most no-bullshit executives do not take pleasure in hurting others for the sake of hurting them. However, they may take some pleasure from calling someone out on what they see as their less than acceptable performance. The pain they inflict is usually a side effect of their reaction to what they see as a significant threat.

SELF-ESTEEM

No-bullshit executives may be capable and competent, but they often have underlying doubts about their competence. They secretly—perhaps unconsciously—fear that they are not the real thing and are in danger of being judged as incompetent when anything goes wrong. This is sometimes referred to as *imposter syndrome.* They fear they are in over their head and that others can see that. Their defensive reaction is to (consciously or not) attack.

HIGH EXPECTATIONS

Almost all no-bullshit executives have incredibly high expectations of themselves. Most have a critical, even reprimanding inner voice when they have not lived up to their own expectations. Even in moments of perceived aggression, they are often treating others more gently than they treat themselves.

IT'S PROBABLY NOT PERSONAL

A subset of no-bullshit executives are primarily committed to knowledge, competence, and mastery. These people have little or a highly selective need for emotional connection, emotional support, or socializing in general. Their communication is unemotional and analytical. People with solid self-esteem are not threatened; people with a higher need for connection or with doubts about their own competence may experience this emotional distance as disrespectful and abrasive.

THE TYPES OF NO-BULLSHIT EXECUTIVES

In my experience, there are four types of no-bullshit executives.

THE WARRIOR

The meaning of the term *warrior* has changed over time. In hunter-gather societies, it had a much narrower meaning. We might typically think of the term applying to our military, police, and firefighters. I am using the term to mean someone who is laser focused on completing the mission and achieving optimal results. They have an uncommon desire to succeed, and they are forged by adversity. Their core values are responsibility, loyalty, mastery, service, and accountability. Almost always, they have purpose and live an altruistic life.

Although I am focusing on the rare master leaders and executives in business, government, and nonprofit organizations, the term applies to people like Martin Luther King Jr., Golda Meir, Mahatma Gandhi, John McCain, Ruth Bader Ginsberg and Margaret Thatcher.

For no-bullshit executives who are warriors, their commitment to service motivates them to learn the people skills necessary to create a high-performance environment. Underneath it all, they are more committed to the mission and the organization than they are to themselves. Their superiors, peers, and reports know that they care enough about people and about relationships to be trusted. Even when they are relentlessly driving for results, most people do not feel disrespected or demeaned. Their high-performing colleagues and reports who value achievement and "getting it right" feel respected, supported, coached, and mentored.

Two of my favorite current examples of this rare leader are Jethro Gibbs on *NCIS* and Hetty Lange on *NCIS Los Angeles*. Both characters exhibit a passionless stare in response to anything less than an unwavering focus on the goal and on results. That same stare is their response to lackadaisical performance, rationalizing, and whining. Most importantly, what they actually say is about challenging their reports to get it right. They do not say things that are insulting or demeaning. Frank Furillo is an older example for those who came of age watching television when I did. Furillo was the tough, demanding police captain on *Hill Street Blues*, who wanted answers and wanted them fast. He did not accept rationalizations for failure to perform. But when one of his young cops needed support or guidance, he could drop the stoic demeanor and act as a mentor.

These leaders may not do much supporting and coaching, but they do enough that they develop their team. If you want a team of high performers, you must respect them and their expertise. Most high performers will leave if they are not respected.

If you are one of these rare executives or leaders, you generate loyalty from the people who work for you. It is unlikely that others will experience you to be disrespectful, and consequently, you are unlikely to receive complaints. In rare cases, people who are insecure or manipulative may file complaints against you, but an investigation will almost always find that you did nothing wrong.

It is more likely that you are not perfect in your management of your human emotions. You may occasionally express frustration, impatience, and anger in a way that crosses the line into disrespect (depending on the culture in which you are operating). Some of your behavior may be driven by getting your way, getting recognition, or some other less altruistic motivation. Assuming these are occasional, you will likely be understood, accepted, and, in the rare cases you are disrespectful, forgiven. Lapses that are occasional and repaired are usually tolerable to others and can produce growth for all.

Especially if you catch yourself and apologize, occasional displays of human imperfection will cause only minimal, temporary upset. They are not likely to have a negative impact on your workgroup or your career.

THE SCIENTIST

This second type of executive is often as committed to results as the warrior. Like the warrior, scientists are typically imperfect in their management of human emotion. They may also be motivated by getting their way or by getting recognition.

The scientist's core values are knowledge, competence, and mastery. Their *why* is about understanding how the world and the universe work. Their *how* is likely to include solving highly complex problems, either for their own sake or to be of service to others. They are more likely to want to get the right answer than to drive results with an even slightly imperfect answer.

Scientists are often selective about personal (emotional) involvement with people. They typically develop deep relationships with a few people but keep a level of emotional distance with most others. It's not that they don't like people. It's that they may not want to connect on a personal level when they believe their purpose at work is to get things done. They are energized by solving complex technical problems to achieve important goals rather than building relationships, supporting, and coaching. Many scientist types also feel drained when they have too much interaction with other people. This is what is referred to as *introversion*.

The scientist often works well with people who do not want or require more than minimal emotional connection with the people they work for and with. However, these executives may create a range of negative reactions from their reports, peers, and superiors, whose brains are wired for and energized by a higher level of emotional connection. The scientist may negatively affect people raised in a family, community, or country where failure to interact with them as people is considered disrespectful. These people will often be less productive and may file complaints.

If you are this type of no-bullshit executive, your reports, peers, and superiors with solid personal self-esteem will likely experience you as someone they can trust, who is a valuable asset to the company. They may also think you are "different" or even a bit odd. Although they prefer more connection in their work relationships, they are generally comfortable with you and pleased to have you around.

When your peers, reports, and superiors do not have solid

self-esteem, you are more likely to receive complaints of harassment, discrimination, and a hostile work environment. Technically speaking, their reactions are not your fault. However, they present a significant leadership and management challenge to you in creating a high-performing team.

At each successive level in an organization, whether that be business, government, military, or nonprofit, success becomes increasingly based on your ability to create trust and buy-in with others. Along with having a strategic vision and technical competence, your ability to create a culture where people feel valued and respected is a critical factor for success.

One way to think about this is that your brain is an operating system, and you need to communicate with other operating systems that are programmed differently. Just as when moving to a different part of the world, you need to learn enough of the language to communicate, and you need to respect the culture. A minor change in mindset, along with a few new interpersonal skills, will make a big difference. You do not have to do a lot, but you do have to do the least you can do.

THE ABRASIVE EXECUTIVE

The third type, the abrasive executive, may or may not be committed to achieving optimal results or serving. In some cases, abrasive executives are more focused on getting their way, status, and recognition. In my experience, despite their human imperfections, their *why* may be the same or similar to those of the warrior, the scientist, or some combination of the two. Their self-esteem is often connected with being the best, achieving great things, or serving others. Because they are so focused on—and impatient about—being the best, achieving great results, or serving others, they often increase the likelihood of things going wrong by failing to accurately assess the time and resources necessary to accomplish complex tasks.

Abrasive behavior is in a gray area between the normal, occasional human behavior of expressing frustration, impatience, and anger and the more damaging behavior of the fourth type: the bully, who we'll discuss in detail in a moment.

The activities that link the two types include verbal abuse, threatening, intimidating, and demeaning communication. The abrasive executive crosses the line into behaviors that their reports, peers, and superiors identify as disrespectful, harmful, and even bullying. The primary difference between executives identified as abrasive and those identified as bullies is the frequency and intensity of the behavior and the intent to do harm.

The abrasive executive is often not aware of the level of pain and damage that others are experiencing. They do not define what they are doing and saying as personal. They feel that if others are reacting, it is a sign of those people's weakness or political correctness.

However, the impact on the organization and the people around them can be as harmful as that of *the bully*, who gets pleasure from creating pain, despite the difference in intention.

If you are an abrasive executive, this book will help you make the relatively minor changes in mindset and develop the skills to manage strong judgment and emotion so others do not experience you as demeaning and harmful.

The foundation of what you must do is to make a commitment

that you will demonstrate respectful, compassionate behavior to all people, whether or not they are exhibiting behavior that you respect. You need to make this commitment because you decide it is the right thing to do, not because you have to protect yourself in our litigious and overprotective environment. You have to find the intrinsic motivation, or the change won't stick.

THE BULLY

In my experience, only 1% to 2% of people fall into this category. Like the abrasive executive, the bully may or may not be committed to achieving optimal results. They may be committed to serving a select cause or group of people. True *bullies* differ from the abrasive executive in the frequency and intensity of their behavior and in their intent to do harm. However, many executives who are identified as bullies actually belong in the abrasive executive category. Abrasive executives may feel justified and gratified by expressing their true opinion to someone who, they believe, deserves it. But their core intention is not to cause pain. They are often shocked when they discover the level of pain experienced by others.

The Workplace Bullying Institute defines bullying as "repeated, health-harming mistreatment of one or more persons (the targets) by one or more perpetrators." *Health-harming* is a key component, leading to lost time, higher medical costs, and employee turnover. The behavior of executives identified both as abrasive and as bullies can rise to meet this definition. The impact of the behavior may be the same. What distinguishes people who are abrasive from people who are bullies is whether they have the intention to and derive pleasure from inflicting harm.

According to the Workplace Bullying Institute, the behavior includes "conduct that is

- Threatening, humiliating, or intimidating, or
- Work interference—sabotage—which prevents work from getting done, or
- Verbal abuse."

Bullying behavior can result in significant costs to the employer, the target, and the executive engaging in the behavior. In many parts of the world, bullying is illegal. While not currently illegal in most of the United States, abrasive behavior can result in complaints, grievances, and costly lawsuits when directed at someone who is in a protected class.

Even if you win the grievance or lawsuit, proving that you are an equal-opportunity bully is expensive and can ruin your career. Like a charge of child abuse or sexual harassment, the charge is enough to ruin you even if you are exonerated.

After a self-assessment, if you find that you get pleasure from causing harm to others, you may not want to give up that pleasure to change. If you have a *why* or core value that making this change is the right thing to do, making the change may be as challenging as maintaining sobriety for an addict, but it can be done.

KEY POINT

Throughout the book are reminders that treating people respectfully does not mean failure to hold them accountable for poor performance and unprofessional behavior. It does not mean letting them off the hook. It simply means identifying performance gaps, communicating expectations and consequences, and following through in a respectful or, ideally, a compassionate tone. Anything less than warrior behavior can—and likely will—create an unintended negative impact on results. Treating people respectfully while still holding them accountable creates significantly better results than treating them with disrespect. And put simply, it is also the right thing to do on a number of levels.

If you are a no-bullshit executive, especially a warrior or a scientist, your relentless focus on results and excellence is both your strength and an invaluable asset to your company or organization. This is not about giving that up.

But if you frequently exhibit behavior others find offensive and abrasive, you have some work to do on that aspect of yourself. There are two pieces of good news. The first is that you do not have to become a different person. You need to make enough change in your communication, perhaps 10%–15%, so that you mitigate the unintended negative impact of your style. The second is that changing your style in this way will make you even more effective and, in reality, tougher. People will not be able to dismiss your expectations and feedback by saying, "What a jerk!"

CHAPTER 3

TAKE YOUR WARRIOR SPIRIT TO THE NEXT LEVEL OF EXECUTIVE SUCCESS

I f you are an abrasive executive, I respect and honor your warrior spirit, but you are not a warrior yet. The best warriors in the world are not abrasive; they are tough. There is a difference. Your mindset is most likely about being a tough-minded, goal-driven leader, focused on production and committed to not wasting time with a lot of needless discussion when you know what needs to be done. And you are likely to believe that developing the kind of communication style described in this book is a waste of time and a lot of politically correct bullshit.

As a no-bullshit executive, you want proof. You will not do something simply because it sounds good. You resent having to follow the orders of superiors simply because they have a bigger badge. You challenge the advice of so-called experts who have not been in the trenches. And you get frustrated that so many people don't "get it." Well, I have been an abrasive executive, and I have years of experience in the trenches with other abrasive executives, partnering with them to mitigate threats to their careers while increasing their influence and results. So here's the challenge: How do you measure up to the best warriors in the world? You have some, perhaps even most, of their qualities, but you likely would not be reading this book or be a candidate for coaching if you possessed them all.

I learned a great deal about what makes a great warrior when I became a volunteer coach for The Honor Foundation (THF) at the suggestion of a colleague. I had never heard of THF, but as soon as he told me about them, I knew I wanted to get involved.

Originally formed to serve the Navy SEALs, THF now serves the entire US Special Operations community: Navy SEALs and Special Warfare Combatant-craft Crewmen, Army Green Berets and Rangers, Marine Raiders, and Air Force Pararescue and Combat Controllers.

Part of what caught my attention is their mission statement and their purpose. THF describes their program as "laser focused on the transition of Navy SEALs and Special Operators. . . . We are a unique transition institute for a unique set of talented Fellows." They have one of the most powerful purpose statements I have seen: "To serve others with Honor for life. So that their next mission is clear and continues to impact the world." One of the key points of this book is that your purpose statement or your *why* is critical to people trusting and accepting your leadership.

I never served in the military. I was not raised in a family of frontline warriors, although my father was a medic who hit the beach in Normandy on the day after D-Day. I saw THF as a way of serving those who had served our country, and a voice in my head said, "You should do this."

My interaction with special operators has given me new perspective regarding my own leadership and followership and those of the executives who are identified as abrasive who I work with. The US Special Operations Forces are direct, tough, and uncompromising. They are not polite and politically correct with each other. Yet, somehow, they form teams that are more like families ("tribes" is how they refer to themselves), and these teams are more effective than any in the world.

Below, I have abstracted some (though not all) of the commitments within the SEALs' ethos and have presented them as a leadership checklist. I have included the ones that apply to the business arena as well as their world.

Be honest as you look at yourself and these commitments. I challenge you to make your own personal assessment and to show it to your trusted superiors, peers, and colleagues and to your family and close friends as well. See how they think you stack up. I have clarified each item after the list. Please review these and put a check mark next to each one that you believe you completely fulfill, and make a note about the ones you need to work on. Compare your assessment with the way you are seen by those you work and live with.

WARRIOR SELF-ASSESSMENT ASSESSMENT

☐ **I have an uncommon desire to succeed.**

☐ **I am forged by adversity.**

☐ **I demand discipline.**

☐ **I expect innovation.**

☐ **I have uncompromising integrity.**

☐ **I expect to lead and be led.**

☐ **I will never quit.**

☐ **I humbly serve.**

☐ **The ability to control my emotions and my actions, regardless of circumstance, sets me apart.**

☐ **I lead by example in all situations.**

☐ **I place the welfare and security of others before my own.**

☐ **I defend those who are unable to defend themselves.**

☐ **I will draw on every remaining ounce of strength to protect my teammates and to accomplish our mission.**

Uncommon Desire to Succeed

Do you set challenging, if not impossible, goals and go after them relentlessly? Do even the top performers wonder where you get your energy and how you keep your focus?

Forged By Adversity

When things go wrong, do you complain or do you press forward, letting the challenges strengthen your resolve?

Discipline

The people who work for nonmilitary organizations usually do not have the same level of motivation as that required by our special forces operators. This is largely because they do not have to overcome huge barriers to entry, and they are living in a culture that allows or even encourages them to act on individual needs above those of the team.

In addition, in the special operations forces, discipline is important because the mission and lives are at stake. Warrior executives want discipline because of things greater than themselves. Some abrasive executives and bullies want discipline because they like having the power to make people jump. Where do you fall?

Innovation

In his book *Team of Teams*, General Stanley McChrystal describes how frontline people must know the big, strategic picture so that when things do not go as planned (as is always the case), they can innovate in the field. This is especially true against incredibly fluid organizations like Al Qaeda. He makes the point that, in the age of the Internet, large, complex corporations and businesses cannot adapt quickly enough to be successful against much smaller, entrepreneurial challengers. Empowering those on the front lines to make decisions makes the organization more agile.

To what degree do you expect to make all the strategic decisions and have rigid adherence to "the way I told you to do it"?

Uncompromising Integrity

General Norman Schwarzkopf famously said, "Leadership is a potent combination of strategy and character. If you must be without one, be without the strategy." The warrior type of no-bullshit executive is outstanding in this area.

Many of the executives I know who get labeled abrasive or as bullies are outstanding in maintaining integrity. But their commitment to saying what they believe to be true—what they see as *telling it like it is*—is a big part of what gets them in trouble.

27

continued

However, I have certainly met no-bullshit executives who do not have a high level of integrity. They can fall into any of the categories but the warrior.

Lead and Be Led

I was a participant in a leadership development program called "The Looking Glass Experience" at the Center for Creative Leadership. During this intense business simulation, I had an *aha* that I had not been a good follower throughout my life. I had only been willing to follow if I agreed with the leader. I realized that this, in part, was why others experienced me as abrasive. This is not being a good team player. As a player, you have to execute the play the coach calls to the best of your ability, even when you would have called something different under the circumstances.

The most elite teams are composed of warriors who are also willing to be led, even when they have a different perspective than the actual leader. This is partly about another of the SEALs' ethos: "My loyalty is beyond reproach."

Perseverance

My understanding of what this means to special operators is that they will endure whatever physical and emotional hardship they must face to complete their mission and to protect the lives of their team and others who cannot protect themselves. Winston Churchill famously said, "It is not enough that we do our best; sometimes we must do what is required." I have not faced such a situation, but I have not quit on anything that I thought was important. There is no question that I would have accomplished more had I not allowed myself to lose focus from time to time. But more than losing focus, if you lose drive or become angry when things don't go as planned, this is a challenge for you.

Humble Service

For most abrasive executives, as well as for most people, displaying humility is a challenge. Lack of humility shows up as pride, arrogance, haughtiness, and pretentiousness. As I mentioned earlier, many executives experienced as abrasive and bullies react to the less-than-perfect results of their reports, peers, and even superiors with impatience, frustration, and sometimes demeaning behavior. Because their self-esteem is attached to being the best and/or being right, achieving great things, and serving others, these reactions, at core, are a defense against situations that threaten their self-esteem.

One of the biggest challenges for executives who aspire to be warriors is to demonstrate the level of humility required by the special operations community. If you think you are the smartest person in the room—and you may well be—and treat people as your inferiors, this will not sit well with those people. You will make it more difficult to get the job done. You are likely to trigger an attitude of *If you're so smart and can do it better, do it yourself!*

Self-Control

Controlling our emotions can be difficult for all of us. It is especially difficult for those of us who are identified as abrasive for the reasons mentioned above. To reemphasize the point, these include:

- Believing that being respectful (dancing around the truth) to people who are not thinking clearly, not performing, or acting without integrity is a bunch of politically correct bullshit,

- Reacting to other people's failure to perform as a personal attack, and

- Being raised in a family or culture where your communication style is normal and accepted.

An additional reason that controlling your emotions and actions is difficult is that by the time we are adults, our way of responding is wired into our brain.

continued

Leadership by Example

Anger and heated statements from the leader tend to increase these in others. In some offices, that way of interaction becomes the norm. New hires see that it is OK to treat others this way and forget simple courtesies such as please, thank you, excuse me, and I'm sorry. You can change not only your behavior but the behavior of your entire workplace by being the model of behavior that creates a great team.

Self-Sacrifice

We live in a culture that has mixed messages about sacrifice. Both personal worth and success may be defined by your title and your income, even if they were achieved by creating damage to colleagues, customers, and the environment. This is an area that provides a great challenge for those executives who want to be among the greatest warriors on the planet.

Defend Others

The US special operations community takes an oath to defend others who cannot defend themselves. Obviously, we live in a culture with mixed messages on this. We do have companies and organizations focused on providing valued services and minimizing if not eliminating damage to others and the environment. However, there are business and other organizations that make decisions with a negative—even destructive—impact on people outside the organization, including clients, customers, and the general public.

Within the organization, there is a reality-based reason for protecting people who are unable to defend themselves. All business and organizational systems have some level of dysfunction. The more dysfunctional they are, the more people are blamed for systems design issues they do not control. Many middle managers are sitting in front of a river of problems that they do not have the authority or the resources to address. I work with them to identify what they do control and the systems issues that need to be addressed without blaming others.

This is not a suggestion that you should ignore inappropriate, unprofessional, or incompetent behavior. It is a suggestion that you consider your own role in creating a system that may not be able to produce consistent results.

Protecting Your Team

This one is difficult in our business culture. In special operations culture, the barriers to entry are so high that, by the time you are functioning as a team, commitment, trust, and competence are quite high. In business, people are hired and promoted without this level of testing. Therefore, protecting all members of the team—in the sense of keeping them on the team—may not be appropriate.

Beyond that, there is no clear ethos in our culture that says you protect your team members who have passed the entry barriers and have demonstrated their commitment and competence. I have met senior executives who truly do their best to protect everyone, and I have met those who will raise their own interest above the team. Can you make the tough choices of when it may be necessary to let a team member go? And are you willing to go the distance to protect worthy team members when it may be politically expedient to let them take the blame?

WARRIOR TEAM LEADERSHIP

The training of the SEALs and their counterparts in the other branches of the armed forces emphasizes the need to collaborate and trust the team. During training, SEALs are required to eat with a buddy so they get used to the idea that they are never alone. Somewhat counterintuitively, this dependence on each other helps develop their ability to make independent decisions.

We were raised in a culture where John Wayne, Clint Eastwood, and Chuck Norris always did better going it alone than waiting for their team to catch up. In the real world, it rarely works that way. As Harry Truman famously said, "It's amazing what you can accomplish if you don't care who gets the credit."

The same thing happens in sports, when too many star players can be detrimental to the team. When Walter Meyer (this book's coauthor) was playing in the intramural handball doubles tournament as an undergrad at Penn State, each dorm floor was allowed to send two teams. On Walt's floor were Rick and Steve, who had both finished in the top five in the handball singles tournament, so it seemed natural to pair them up for doubles. They would be a great team—two of the top players at the university would be an unbeatable pair, right?

Walt and Bud had both finished way down in the singles tournament and would be the floor's B team. But a strange thing happened. Although Rick or Steve could easily beat Walt or Bud at singles, as a team, Walt and Bud could beat Rick and Steve every time. Rick and Steve were each sure they were the best to handle every shot, so they chased the ball all over the court, often dueling each other for position. Walt and Bud became interdependent and reasoned that either of them handling the shot was better than competing for it.

The A team of Rick and Steve was knocked out of the doubles tournament early, while Walt and Bud finished fourth out of the hundreds of teams entered. Sometimes, it is more effective to have two competent players working together than two superstars working at cross-purposes. I believe Shaq and Kobe had the same problem for a while.

For a team to be successful over the long term, it needs to truly be a team, not an individual or collection of superstars. Notice how many NBA or NFL teams fall apart when their star player is injured? They did not have a great team; they had a great player and a supporting cast. Although they may win in the short term, they are vulnerable if anything happens to their lynchpin. Remember the US Olympic basketball team in 2004: The best players in the world were on that squad, but they lost when they went up against a less talented group who played like a team instead of as individuals.

WARRIORS LEADING WARRIORS

McChrystal writes that when the US Special Forces were able to organize to be more adaptive, they started doing better instead of always being several moves behind. In fact, their senior leadership changed the way they managed: They kept the entire teams informed of the bigger picture rather than doling out individual orders and expecting blind acceptance. This allowed their teams to make strategic decisions when reality did not match the plan.

To truly have a team, you must respect the skills and abilities of the other members to execute their part of the plan. This means letting everyone in on the goals for the initiative or project and the strategic information driving it so that, as the situation shifts, they can shift in a way that pursues the goals, even if it was not in the original plan.

The way this works is, once a plan is proposed, you invite everyone on the team or anyone affected by the project to find flaws in the proposal. My first coach, Louis Spain, had a term for this: the *shoot-it-down* technique. (In today's environment, I now call this the *What am I missing?* technique.) Leaders often get so caught up in their own assumptions and beliefs about what is happening that they forget that everyone on their team, from the top to the bottom, has information they do not have.

Strangely enough, one way to get better performance out of your team is to stop acting like its leader. General McChrystal wrote that the SEALs and their cohorts conducted a mission review in which they eliminated rank. Anyone was allowed to tell anyone else they had messed up. (My understanding is that, since the general's departure, this type of exercise does not happen as frequently.) McChrystal said this was done in an honest, forthright way that included language not acceptable in the business world. Everyone's life was at stake.

McChrystal provides another example of the importance of the ability to deal directly with others regardless of rank. Following a tragic airline disaster that could have been averted had the pilot not been the only one allowed to direct the action, the airline industry adopted *crew resource management* solutions. The pilot is still in overall command, but others may speak freely about action that must be taken immediately. When lives are on the line, it doesn't help to have only one person making decisions when that person has too many decisions to make each second and cannot possibly be able to keep track of all the things happening at once.

This sort of adaptive training is credited with saving the 155 lives aboard US Airways Flight 1549, when Captain Sullenberger and his crew managed a miracle in setting their crippled plane down on the Hudson River. In the less than two minutes of flight time left to them, the crew didn't have time to discuss procedures or follow checklists. All they could do was act.

In the business environment, teams are far more effective when everyone can speak honestly and directly. As the boss, you should ask for direct feedback. Your reports and peers should be encouraged to tell you when they think you are missing something or when you're wrong. This will encourage others to be direct with you. "This is what I am thinking of doing. Tell me: What am I missing?"

Your life may never have to depend on input from your subordinates, but your company or career might, so you would be well served to not intimidate your people so badly that they will not give you the advice or information you need when you need it. As Arnold H. Glasgow wrote, "A good leader takes a little more than his [or her] share of the blame, a little less than his [or her] share of the credit." In the book *Good to Great*, the writers found that great leaders went even further and took little of the credit and all of the blame.

REASONS FOR DOING THE LEAST YOU CAN DO

CHAPTER 4

It's Lack of Alignment, Stupid

One of the most frequent triggers of no-bullshit executive behavior that gets identified as abrasive or bullying in the workplace is projects where the team fails to achieve goals, misses deadlines, exceeds budget, or disappoints internal and external customers and stakeholders. These types of failure may appear to be the incompetence of the team, but they may actually be a failure of leadership to align the team to the organization's mission and goals as well as its value chain.

In many corporations, businesses, and organizations, the top executives rightly see their responsibility as developing strategy. However, they often do not remember that creating alignment throughout the value chain is also their responsibility. In my experience, they may request input from an external consultant and several trusted internal stakeholders. But they often fail to systematically collect input from the entire value chain. Too often, input from the stakeholders closest to the customer is not seen as worth taking the time to collect. When, in fact, this input is often one of the keys to success.

Members of the C-suite team know they must reach agreement on and communicate the key strategic goals for their business or organization and the few initiatives that are necessary to achieve these goals. These initiatives are large and cross-functional, involving significant investment in money and staff time. However, this internal consensus is often driven by two to three members of the team who are more powerful and more in favor with the CEO, board, or business owner. There is not true consensus on direction nor alignment on implementation.

Following the achievement of what is perceived as "consensus" on strategic goals, the implementation of the initiative is delegated to a report of one of the key supporters of the initiative. This is often a VP or director, depending on the organizational structure.

Believing that they know what needs to happen, how to do it, and that everyone is swamped so it will be difficult to get key stakeholders together, the project lead decides to work on what they control. The lead does solicit input from a limited number of trusted peers. Often, these are people who have a similar perspective.

Over the first three to nine months or so, this group of people makes decisions about the specific wording of the goal, the underlying strategic assumptions, the measures of success, the necessary resources, and the process for implementation. Typically, they incur significant cost and invest significant amounts of their own and others' time.

After months of investment, they have completed what they believe they can and should do on their own. They start to meet with all the other functions who have to implement what they have designed. In many cases, they hold an overview meeting to brief the other functions on what they need to do. These meetings are followed by individual meetings to create work packets for each of the functions.

This is where the first signs of trouble show up. The stakeholders from the other links in the value chain begin to say (or argue) that the original goal and the strategy are not right, the implementation plan is seriously flawed, or both. The project leads and their C-suite superiors view this as resistance and view the resisters as not as bright or as committed as they are.

The resisters, on the other hand, believe that, once again, senior management has acted without understanding the impact of the changes on end customers and everyone in between. The C-suite team observes this conflict and concludes that their people do not know how to implement projects. It never occurs to them that they didn't do their own job; they failed to check their assumptions about their strategic goals throughout the value chain. It also does not occur to them that their reports do not have the leverage to drive alignment when there is not agreement on the senior team.

At this point, the more abrasive executives get triggered and push the project forward using impatience, anger, threats, and other abrasive behavior. Their belief is that these people don't get how

41

important this is or don't care. If only we had more "this is important; get it done no matter what" personalities on our team, this would not be happening.

This type of ongoing dysfunction creates significant tension. The tension is caused by forcing an implementation across a value chain without checking the reality and impact of the underlying assumptions and implementation tactics with stakeholders in each link of the value chain. The natural tendency is then to blame the most abrasive or passive-aggressive people rather than looking for the root cause of failure to implement.

Recognizing that you operate in a value chain is especially important in large, complex organizations that operate in what is known as a VUCA environment. The term VUCA was introduced by the military to describe environments that contain volatility, uncertainty, complexity, and ambiguity. Creating work cultures where people are aligned with the mission, understand the strategy, and are empowered to make decisions when necessary are critical in VUCA environments. Leaders who encourage a continuous inflow of perspectives and options greatly increase their opportunities for success.

I recommend the book *Direction, Alignment, Commitment: Achieving Better Results Through Leadership* by Cynthia McCauley and Lynn Fick-Cooper. It is based on decades of research by the Center for Creative Leadership (CCL), one of the most respected providers of research on leadership, as well as leadership development programs and executive coaching. CCL says that direction, alignment, and commitment are the three outcomes of effective leadership.

AGILE METHODOLOGY IN THE C-SUITE

You need more than great leadership to get great results. You also need to know how to design and develop processes and solve problems in complex, dynamic environments.

Agile methodology was created as a way to develop large enterprise resource planning (ERP) and other software systems that work. Before agile was introduced, the process for designing and implementing these large, comprehensive systems involved, roughly, the following steps:

1. Interview end users to identify their needs. In a large corporation or medium-sized company, this might take six months to a year.

2. Design the system. This was a 6–18-month process.

3. Spend the next several years fixing everything that did not work.

There are a number of reasons that these large software implementations ran into so many problems prior to agile. These reasons are the same ones that many other cross-functional initiatives achieve suboptimal results or fail. These C-suite-driven initiatives may involve strategy, innovation, design, supply chain, or process improvement.

The reason agile was developed is that these projects occur in constantly changing business, economic, and social environments. With this much change and complexity, there are five core realities:

- It is unlikely that you will correctly articulate the goal and all the measures of success up front.

- It is not possible to know all the specifications up front. The end users don't know what they need until they start using the system.

- Each member of an organization's value chain has information not known by anyone else. Failure to collect information from the entire value chain typically results in missing significant data that might challenge the goal or the implementation strategy.

- Changing a complex system always generates previously unknown information in the form of both obstacles and opportunities. This information usually becomes apparent 6–18 months into the project.

- In a volatile market, there is a good chance that significant aspects of your goal and design will no longer be relevant one to two years after implementation.

Agile is a methodology designed to quickly surface previously unseen information and create a channel for changing goals, strategies, and tactics before millions of dollars and thousands of hours of staff time are spent going in a direction that will not work.

When agile is implemented in a software project, a designated committee of the internal and external customers of the project is assembled and maintains authority to change goals and tactics at any time. The project leads hold daily morning meetings, called *scrums*, which last for 15–30 minutes, for all the implementers to review what was done yesterday in order to communicate decisions that will affect other work groups, bottlenecks, resources needed, or other issues. Often, they let the end users react to or "play with" whatever small piece has been developed in order to get continuous end user direction.

On a weekly basis, there is a longer meeting to review these same issues. These longer meetings often involve the customer team. Then, on a monthly basis, there is another meeting to bring to the surface any information that challenges the original and current assumptions about the goal and about implementation strategy and tactics.

LEAN METHODOLOGY IN THE C-SUITE

I was introduced to lean methodology when I was the chief operations officer of the company I mentioned in chapter 1. You may recall that, in those days, I had even more of a tendency to be abrasive than I do now. A lot of it was frustration around cross-functional initiatives that did not achieve their goals.

One of my close friends was dating a man named Louis Spain, who was an expert in continuous process improvement (CPI) at Rohr Industries, a well-known defense contractor. CPI, which has its roots in the pioneering work of W. Edwards Deming, is now referred to as lean and Six Sigma, or the Toyota Method.

At the request of General Westmoreland, who was responsible for helping to rebuild Japan after World War II, Deming introduced CPI to some major Japanese companies, including Toyota. He had also offered his approach to American industry, and especially the American car industry, but there was no interest. You know the rest.

Rather than reading Deming directly, Louis suggested a book called *The Goal* by Eli Goldratt. I started reading at 10:00 one night, intending to read one chapter. I finished at 5:00 in the morning, having had an epiphany: *Stupid, the reason that your people are not successful implementing your projects is that you are not employing a system that works.*

I called Nick Krnich, the owner (and my boss), and let him know I would be late but that I had served him a lot better by finishing the book and would talk to him soon. Fortunately, Nick trusted me. Even more fortunately, he read the book and agreed to hire Louis as our consultant and coach.

Over the next two years, we flowcharted our processes, looking for missing steps, steps that were out of order, and steps that should be eliminated. We also identified parts of the process where everything backed up—bottlenecks. We used the CPI method to collect data in order to identify the root causes of problems in our key systems.

We developed potential solutions and vetted them prior to implementation. Our efficiency and quality improved significantly—so much so that WellPoint Health Networks, a Fortune 500 company, eventually decided to buy our company.

To give you a feel for what this was like, I want to describe something that happened about a year into the process. We were addressing an issue we were having in our medical records system. Our medical records administrator, Lynn, knocked on my office door and asked me to take a look at a flowchart she was working on. This particular chart had gone around the conference room twice, and going through it was the last thing I wanted to do. However, Lynn had saved our butts on numerous occasions; I trusted her judgment and didn't want to say no to her.

Lynn started with step 1 of the problematic process, as we had been taught to do: "The phone rings." The second step was "The receptionist answers the phone." Somewhere about 45 minutes later, Lynn pointed to a step in the flowchart and said, "And then I do this."

I was puzzled and asked, "Why do you do that?"

"Because you told me to do that," she said in a triumphant tone.

"I didn't tell you to do that," I said.

"Yes, you did. Don't you remember two years ago when we had the case where the provider died and we were having difficulty getting the case notes we needed in order to close the case? Well . . . I added some steps into the system to make sure it never happens again. They did increase the steps and time it takes to close a case."

"Lynn, that was a workaround," I said. "It was never my intention to change the system."

I thought, *I can't believe she implemented this.*

I was about to blow my stack at Lynn, but I caught myself instead. I said, "Let's document how we are going to do things going forward." I thanked Lynn for picking up on this, and she left my office.

Fortunately, I realized that my anger should be directed at myself for not having made sure that the system was flowcharted and for not designing a continuous improvement process. In a nutshell, I had given unclear directives and had not requested feedback to assure alignment.

If you have inherited a system and are not at fault for the design, I would argue that it is much more effective to rechannel your anger to fixing the system than at the people who have been directed to operate a flawed system. This misdirected anger happens often, when people curse out the poor phone operator for a flaw in the way their cable company is run. The anger is at the service; it shouldn't be directed at the person who is simply trying to make a living by answering phone calls.

A colleague told me he once started a phone call to a cable company with, "I want to speak to your supervisor."

"Why, sir, is there something wrong?"

"Yes, something is very wrong, and they don't pay you enough to have to listen to what I am about to scream at your supervisor."

The operator laughed and said, "You're right. They don't. I'll transfer you."

In the next chapter, you will find research and arguments about why treating people respectfully when your brain is telling you they do not deserve it is the right thing to do.

CHAPTER 5

HARD AND SOFT POWER, THE BAD-ASS CHICKENS, AND GOOGLE RESEARCH ON TEAMS

I n the special operations community, building trust and credibility is supported by the fact that everyone on the team had to pass the same incredibly difficult barriers to entry. In the business world, many people join the team without a similar baptism of fire. Because of that, people in the business world typically doubt the competence of others, regardless of their title. For executives, that lack of respect translates into distrust, impatience, and a reluctance to clue everyone in on the details of the entire mission, initiative, or project.

Here are some of the things I have regularly heard abrasive executives say to their reports and peers over the years. To be truthful, these are things I have said myself:

- "It's obvious what we need to do. Why are you worrying about whether everyone is happy? This is about doing what is needed to win."

- "Why are you so concerned about every little detail? We need to roll this out quickly."

- "All you do is figure out everything that won't work. Just do it."

- "This is not about changing the world; it's about making money for our stockholders."

These comments have something in common. They all represent only one type of power: hard power.

HARD AND SOFT POWER

The concept of hard and soft power was introduced by Joseph Nye in his book *Bound to Lead: The Changing Nature of American Power*. He said, "When one country gets other countries to want what it wants, it might be called *co-optive* or *soft power*, in contrast with the *hard* or *command power* of ordering others to do what it wants."

In their 1966 book, *The Managerial Grid: Leadership Styles for Achieving Production through People*, and in their succeeding publications,

Robert Blake and Jane Mouton introduced and enhanced a management system called *the grid*, based on hard and soft power, which is applicable to organizations operating in today's VUCA environment.

In the workplace, hard power is about being relentlessly competitive, ambitious, and mission-and goal-focused, driving for results, and holding people accountable. Soft power is about inspiration, service, collaboration, alignment, mentoring, coaching, and support.

In my experience and in the literature on leadership, executives and managers who use an integration of hard and soft power are far more effective in creating a high-performance, customer-focused culture than are those who don't.

No-bullshit executives immediately know the downside of using too much soft power. People who use too much soft power create a variety of unintended consequences, which include negative impacts on quality, customer satisfaction, brand, morale, and revenue. This is because too much soft power often results in a failure to drive goals and objectives, a failure to make tough decisions, and a failure to hold people accountable. All of these result in lowering the morale of the people who care about doing a good job, which creates a further downward spiral.

Exclusive or unbalanced use of hard power, especially combined with frequent abrasive and disrespectful communication, also has significant downsides. The unbalanced use of hard power is a 17th-century military model that works on the battlefield but not in complex environments in which success requires everyone to contribute their intellectual capital. As McChrystal wrote in his book, "The lessons of World War II were not applicable to the fluid wars the US military encountered in Iraq and Afghanistan. When things become increasingly complex, only a response that can shift quickly can stand a chance."

According to McChrystal, "Research suggests that the best teams have collective intelligence. They are not composed of the smartest people but the ones with the best connections among them to be able to share information. A diverse team with diverse backgrounds and experience can often find a wider range of solutions than a homogenous one or a team on which the members are reluctant to share ideas that are different."

People who use too much hard power unintentionally create a negative impact on quality, customer satisfaction, brand, morale, and revenue. In a complex environment, everyone from the C-suite to the frontline customer service people has critical information related to the market, the customer, the operation, and—ultimately—organizational success.

Hard power leaders usually believe that it is their job to analyze the market, determine strategy, delegate implementation, and then hold people accountable. Most assume that they have all the information they need. They typically do not recognize that intelligence exists from other parts of the value chain that might challenge their core assumptions and goals.

In addition to the data, information, and wisdom available throughout the value chain, much previously unknown data becomes available as soon as you change anything. To quote the great sociologist Kurt Lewin, "If you want truly to understand something, try to change it."

In a predominantly hard power system, there is no readily accessible communication channel to the key decision makers. Consequently, they do not receive or listen to the following sorts of information:

- Information that might challenge the underlying assumptions about their initial goals and strategies
- Information that surfaces as a result of implementation (changing things) that challenges their underlying assumptions

The information eventually gets to them, but often only after a large investment of money and staff time. The point is that the reason for soliciting and listening to input from the whole value chain is not to make everyone feel included and respected; that is the side effect. The reason to solicit and listen to information from the whole value chain is that they know things that are critical to your success and the success of the company. Not listening significantly increases the probability that you will fail.

As in the theory of mission review (after-action debriefs in the military), everyone who participated knows something that someone else does not. Learning that key piece could spell the difference between life and death on the next mission.

If your leadership crosses the line from tough-minded and hard power to abrasive and disrespectful, not only will those below you be less likely to share much-needed information, but it will almost certainly create morale problems as well. Some people who feel disrespected react by working harder to get acknowledgment and appreciation. Others become hesitant to speak up, and still others engage in outright sabotage. In any case, you lose out on leveraging the full value of employees' intellectual capital, perspective, and creativity.

The bottom line of all this is that the most effective leaders use both hard and soft power. At times, goal-focused leadership and driving for results with relentless accountability are absolutely required.

At other times, collaboration, systems thinking, support, and development are most effective. The most effective business leaders do at least some of both.

THE BAD-ASS CHICKENS

I once attended a program on the latest western scientific research on mindfulness and compassion cultivation. Stephen Hayes, PhD, introduced us to research conducted by William Muir, a professor at Purdue University who specialized in breeding animals. He referred to this research as the "Bad-Ass Chickens."

I remember Dr. Hayes telling us that Dr. Muir focused on breeding chickens to increase egg productivity. He started with a large population of hens that he placed in cages in groups of nine. He then bred six generations of chickens based on two types of conditions.

Under the first set of conditions, he identified ONLY the hens who produced the most eggs within each cage. He then removed and bred them to produce the next generation of hens. After that, observed their offspring and selected the hens that laid the most eggs and used them to breed the next generation for six generations. He placed their offspring in cages and bred them together. Under the second set of conditions, he chose the groups of hens in the cages that produced the most eggs and bred them together to produce the next generation of offspring. These groups included the hens who laid the most eggs as well as the hens in each group that laid few or no eggs. As with the other condition, he continued for six generations.

In the introduction to an internet interview with Dr. William Muir titled "When the Strong Outbreed the Weak," Dr. David Sloan

Wilson states, "The most productive hen in each cage was the biggest bully, who achieved her productivity by suppressing the productivity of the other hens. Bullying behavior is a heritable trait, and several generations were sufficient to produce a strain of psychopaths." He said that in the other condition involving group selection, "All nine hens are alive and fully feathered. Egg productivity increased 160% in only a few generations, an almost unheard-of response to artificial selection in animal breeding experiments."[1]

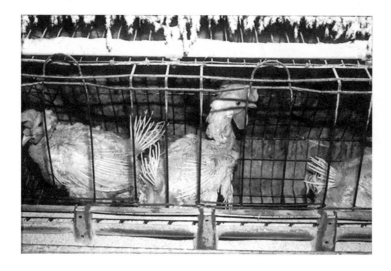

In an article in *The Huffington Post*, Dr. Wilson said, "That's why the second method worked. Selecting the most productive *groups*

1   "When the Strong Outbreed the Weak: An Interview with William Muir," David Sloan Wilson and Dr. William M. Muir, from "This View of Life," The Evolution Institute. https://evolution-institute.org/when-the-strong-outbreed-the-weak-an-interview-with-william-muir/

favored peaceful and cooperative hens, despite their selective disadvantage within groups."[2]

So it would appear that combining hard- and soft- power chickens produces more eggs. Does combining people who exhibit a similar mixture create the best possible team? In other words, are the best producers in the group (the best egg layers) likely to produce the best results if you put them on the same team? Or is production a group trait rather than just an individual trait? (We're back to having all NBA All-Stars on one Olympic team, aren't we?)

---

2   David Sloan Wilson, "Truth and Reconciliation for Group Selection XIV: Group Selection in the Laboratory," *The Huffington Post*, 09/23/2009, Updated May 25, 2011

WHAT GOOGLE LEARNED FROM ITS QUEST TO BUILD THE PERFECT TEAM

If you are not impressed with chicken-breeding experiments, would you be opposed to considering some research conducted at Google to determine how to build the perfect team?

In his 2016 *New York Times Magazine* article called "What Google Learned From Its Quest to Build the Perfect Team," Charles Duhigg presented the background to Google's research called Project Aristotle.

> He said that "software engineers are encouraged to work together, in part because studies show that groups tend to innovate faster, see mistakes more quickly and find better solutions to problems. Studies also show that people working in teams tend to achieve better results and report higher job satisfaction. In a 2015 study, executives said that profitability increases when workers are persuaded to collaborate more. Within companies and conglomerates, as well as in government agencies and schools, teams are now the fundamental unit of organization. If a company wants to outstrip its competitors, it needs to influence not only how people work but also how they work *together*."

In my experience, as well as this research, there is significant evidence that the typical behaviors of no-bullshit executives who are identified as abrasive or bullies are a block to optimal performance and profitability.

Duhigg went on to say—

"In 2012, the company embarked on an initiative—code-named

Project Aristotle—to study hundreds of Google's teams and figure out why some stumbled while others soared. . . .

The company's top executives long believed that building the best teams meant combining the best people.

We are back to the Bad Ass Chickens again.

They discovered "'Some teams had a bunch of smart people who figured out how to break up work evenly,' said Anita Woolley, the study's lead author. 'Other groups had pretty average members, but they came up with ways to take advantage of everyone's relative strengths. Some groups had one strong leader. Others were more fluid, and everyone took a leadership role.'

Abeer Dubey said, 'We had lots of data, but there was nothing showing that a mix of specific personality types or skills or backgrounds made any difference. The *who* part of the equation didn't seem to matter.'"

"As the researchers studied the groups, however, they noticed two behaviors that all the good teams generally shared. First, on the good teams, members spoke in roughly the same proportion, a phenomenon the researchers referred to as 'equality in distribution of conversational turn-taking.' On some teams, everyone spoke during each task; on others, leadership shifted among teammates from assignment to assignment. But in each case, by the end of the day, everyone had spoken roughly the same amount. 'As long as everyone got a chance to talk, the team did well,' Woolley said. 'But if only one person or a small group spoke all the time, the collective intelligence declined.'"

If you are a no-bullshit executive, it is likely that you talk more than anyone else and do not want to be challenged. If you are the scientist, it is likely that you are not interested in people being themselves beyond engaging in challenging, analytical conversation. Hopefully, this provides some intrinsic motivation for you to modify your leadership and communication style beyond "you should be nicer to people."

The second behavior identified by the Google researchers is that the good teams all had high "average social sensitivity"—a fancy way of saying they were skilled at intuiting how others felt based on their tone of voice, their expressions, and other nonverbal cues.

In an *Inc.* article published July 19, 2017, Michael Schneider summarized the five key characteristics of enhanced teams.[3]

- Dependability: Team members get things done on time and meet expectations.

- Structure and clarity: High-performing teams have clear goals and have well-defined roles within the group.

- Meaning: The work has personal significance to each member.

- Impact: The group believes their work is purposeful and positively impacts the greater good.

- Psychological safety: We've all been in meetings and, due to the fear of seeming incompetent, have held back questions or ideas. I get it. It's unnerving to feel like you're in an environment where everything you do or say is under a microscope.

  But imagine a different setting. A situation in which everyone is safe to take risks, voice their opinions, and ask judgment-free questions. A culture where managers provide

---

3 Michael Schneider, "Google Spent 2 Years Studying 180 Teams. The Most Successful Ones Shared These 5 Traits," *Inc.*, July 19, 2017, https://www.inc.com/michael-schneider/google-thought-they-knew-how-to-create-the-perfect.html.

air cover and creat safe zones so employees can let down their guard. That's psychological safety.

Both the "Bad-Ass Chickens" research and the Google research show evidence that the best-performing teams have a mixture of types. These include members who are driven to be productive, and members who are focused on developing others and creating a positive environment. In addition, the Google results indicate that, regardless of the style of the members, the members of the most effective teams all provide roughly equal amounts of input.

But let's be real. Not everyone is equally capable of all types of work. If you find yourself constantly having to work around certain members of your team or find that others want to avoid being stuck with a certain person on the team, take a good look at that person. They may have other skills that can be better used in a different capacity. Or, perhaps, they do not belong on the team at all.

If you are one of those people who uses too much hard power, you can increase your effectiveness by integrating some soft power tools. You do not want to eliminate your tough-minded approach. Integration of soft power tools will increase your impact, and paradoxically, others will experience you as even tougher.

Studies have shown that people who are willing to apologize and admit mistakes are not only *not* viewed as weak; they are actually perceived in a better light. (My colleague, author, and expert consultant Cynthia Burnham warns me that this might not be true for women in all cultures.) This includes demonstrating courage, integrity, and humility rather than blaming others when they contributed to or caused the problem.

CHAPTER 6

CHARLES DARWIN, NEUROSCIENCE, AND THE MARTIAL ARTS

Additional research suggests that treating people you do not like or respect in a respectful and compassionate manner is in your best interest because, not only is it the least you can do, but from a bottom-line perspective, you will get better results. In order to help you decide whether treating these people with respect and compassion is consistent with your core values, I will offer some philosophical and spiritual arguments that emanate from Charles Darwin, Western science, and the martial arts. I hope this chapter will help you gain clarity on what is in it for you to make a commitment to change the way you communicate and on what you need to do to achieve your goal.

CHARLES DARWIN

At an executive coaching conference years ago, I heard keynote speaker Joel Barker, a futurist, author, and filmmaker, say something that significantly clarified my thinking about leadership: "Charles Darwin did not originally say 'survival of the fittest,'" Barker told the audience. It was said by Herbert Spenser. I understood Barker to say that Darwin's meaning would be better understood as 'survival of the most fit.'

The distinction is profound: *Fittest* is widely misinterpreted to mean "most able to conquer others." What Darwin meant, in borrowing the phrase from English philosopher and social scientist Herbert Spencer, is "most adaptable." Those who can adapt to their environment are most likely to survive. It isn't the *strongest* who survive, but the most able to *change.*

Barker went on to say that Spenser's statement "survival of the fittest" was used to justify colonialism (conquering others). Bullies, who enjoy creating pain for others, or abrasive executives, who are better intentioned, may use the same rationalization to justify their behavior. They believe that the laws and protections that are afforded to employees run counter to the forces of natural selection. "If only government regulators would get out of the way and allow businesses to compete and win."

To be clear, when there is a fire burning and you are the only one who smells the smoke, you must do something to create focus, urgency, and anxiety. Those of us who work with executives to change the culture of their company know that change will not occur unless the key influencers are significantly more uncomfortable staying the same than they are facing the stress and uncertainty of change. We refer to this as *creating a burning platform*. People jump from burning buildings when the fear of the flames outweighs their fear of the height.

In my humble (not legal) opinion, as someone who has brain wiring that creates abrasive communication, I believe that many of the laws and protections afforded employees have the unintended negative consequence of protecting less-than-honorable people who have learned how to play the system. However, I have come to believe that even when dealing with dishonorable people, I am more effective when I address the lack of integrity and the negative impact of their behavior rather than disparage the person.

Before leaving this topic, I want to ask, "What do you think Charles Darwin said is the most import instinct for survival of the human species?" Most people respond "aggression."

In fact, Charles Darwin said that the most important instinct for the survival of the human species is *sympathy*. The human infant requires more nurturing than any other infant in nature. Without sympathy, the human species would not survive. Survival was also driven by sensitivity to one's family group or tribe. This is reflected in the willingness of tribe members to die for another member who was threatened.

According to psychologist Paul Ekman, Darwin also described how natural selection favored the evolution of compassion, regardless of what originally motivated such behavior: "In however complex a manner this feeling may have originated, as it is one of high importance to all those animals which aid and defend one another, it will have been increased through natural selection; for those communities, which included the greatest number of the most sympathetic members, would flourish best and rear the greatest number of offspring."[4]

The research that Google did is consistent with Ekman's point. The best-performing teams have one thing in common: They create an environment where it is safe to be yourself.

YOUR BRAIN 1: THE FIGHT–FREEZE–FLIGHT RESPONSE

As I stated before, the self-esteem of most no-bullshit executives is connected to their ability to be the best, achieve outstanding results, and to serve others. To feel good about themselves, they need to demonstrate expertise and competence and to be recognized and respected by others. That is why they are willing to jump over the many obstacles and roadblocks within the business and production systems of their companies, to say nothing of experiencing and adjusting to the personalities of the people they work with.

For many high-driving, achievement-oriented people, mistakes and failure on projects trigger the same physiological response that is triggered if their life were to be threatened by someone holding a knife to their throat in a dark alley. This response was described by Hans Selye in 1936 and is known as the *fight–freeze–flight* response.

In recent years, scientists and psychologists have been discussing

---

4 Charles Darwin, *The Descent of Man, and Selection in Relation to Sex.* 1871.

the potential that there also might be an ingrained response to threat that they refer to as *tend–befriend*. If it exists, I understand this to mean that some people are hardwired to use soft power in response to an attack.

When the fight–freeze–flight response is triggered, the body is flooded with neurotransmitters, which prepare you to survive the attack by fighting, running, or freezing (or, perhaps, tending or befriending). These neurotransmitters increase heart rate, respiration, and perspiration. The blood flows away from the surface of the body (creating cold hands and feet) as a survival mechanism if you are cut. The part of your brain that engages in higher-level thinking (the prefrontal cortex) closes down so that you are operating on instinct (referred to as the *reptilian brain*), which drives your most-practiced (ingrained) behavior patterns, whether or not they are effective responses in your environment.

If you are attacked in an alley, the fight–freeze–flight response may be lifesaving if you have martial arts skills. However, if your attacker is more skilled in the martial arts, running or giving up your wallet may prove more beneficial than trying to resist.

In the workplace, the fight–freeze–flight response to a real or imagined threat can drive either positive or negative results. If you are not skilled at managing your response, your communication will often show up as abrasive or bullying behavior. If you are conflict avoidant or passive-aggressive, you might appear to lack confidence or, perhaps, to be dishonest. Neither of these contributes to a positive perception of your leadership ability or your promotability. If your core purpose involves being a good human being, you may also lack integrity in your own estimation.

The fight–freeze–flight response can produce beneficial results for you, your team, and the business. This will occur if, like the master martial artist, you have the self-control and interpersonal skills to manage it. You must have developed the ability to remain calm and focused in the face of a verbal threat or attack, and you must have a repertoire of powerful but respectful things you can say. When you are prepared, your prefrontal cortex does not close down in the heat of battle, limiting your ability to respond strategically and appropriately.

An unmanaged fight–freeze–flight response almost always has the impact of decreasing the respect others have for you. They may see you as lacking maturity, respect, manners, and compassion in the case of abrasive behavior, or integrity, courage, and honor in the case of passive-aggressive behavior. (As a side note, operating at that high-adrenaline level is also hard on your body. There are negative health effects to being in fight–freeze–flight mode too much.)

Unless you have unusual leverage within the business, these responses will negatively affect your career. If you are the "abrasive as hell" owner of a company, although no one can fire or discipline you, you will experience a toll in employee turnover and customers who no longer wish to do business with you.

YOUR BRAIN 2: NEURAL PATHWAYS, THE WIRING IN YOUR BRAIN

Current research suggests that our responses to any situation (stimulus) are driven by neural pathways activating in our brain. For instance, if you experience someone challenging you as a threat, your neural pathways will conduct an electrical impulse to the part of your brain that triggers the fight–freeze–flight response. If you worked to change your thinking and reactions to view someone challenging you as an opportunity to get information, a different set of neural pathways would become energized.

We also know that neurons that fire together, wire together. Neural pathways develop as a response to genetic predisposition and to experience, both external and internal. External experience is everything in our environment. Internal experience consists of the thoughts, feelings, and behaviors we create. Over time, our experience creates ingrained, habitual responses. Therefore, changing our responses requires awareness and practice.

Years ago, I heard a metaphor that describes the challenge of changing our behavior driven by large neural pathways. Because I cannot remember who said it, you are getting a paraphrased version. Imagine you are driving a car at 150 miles per hour on a superhighway and you hit a deer crossing the road. You might say, "In the future, I will not hit the deer." But at 150 MPH on a superhighway, you do not have enough time to make an alternative decision, and you will certainly hit the deer, should the same situation arise again.

To avoid hitting the deer, you must build another road (a new set of neural pathways). When people first try to change what they notice and how they react, it feels like they are hacking their way out of a rainforest with a dull machete. It's not easy to blaze new paths—in the jungle or in your brain.

The good news is that changing your reaction is less difficult than you might think. In my experience—making this type of change myself and helping people in executive coaching make such changes—it takes about three months of practice to create the real-time choice allowing you to select a different response than the one conditioned by the previously existing neural pathways.

Changing habitual behavior comes in small steps. The first step is to commit to changing and to develop a vision of what the change will look and feel like. Then you focus to increase your awareness when you are thinking, feeling, and behaving in ways you want to change. You then create alternative responses and practice using them. Over time, you are able to shift in real time. Finally, you develop what might be referred to as muscle memory, and the new behavior becomes automatic. In my personal experience, the old habits remain and still show up from time to time. It is a journey.

For most people, changing old habits requires a minimum of several hours per week, which represents somewhere between a small and medium investment of time for a busy executive. For someone with your commitment and focus, the time period to see real-time results may be much shorter.

Through the use of FMRI technology, scientists have studied people who meditate or who practice what is now referred to as *mindfulness*. The implication of the research is that you can rewire your brain if you are currently wired to say disrespectful things under stress, threat, or attack. Some scientists believe there is evidence that you can develop new neural pathways by changing your thinking, emotions, behavior, and focus.

In the 1970s, Jon Kabat-Zinn developed Mindfulness-Based Stress Reduction (MBSR). He integrated the practices of yoga and Buddhist masters with Western scientific practices. In the last 20 years or more, a collaboration among science, psychology, social science, and the contemplative traditions is developing and evolving the practice of mindfulness.

Although the science is in its early stages, it has progressed enough that many health plans, medical centers, and hospitals across the United States and Europe offer programs based on this evolving research.

Mindfulness and, as I discuss in the next chapter, a related practice called *compassion cultivation*, have helped me shift my own tendency to be triggered by what my brain wiring refers to as "people who do not deserve compassion and respect." Through these practices, I have increased my ability to notice my fight–freeze–flight response before it gets strong enough to trigger abrasive communication. I then developed and practiced different thinking and emotional responses to the situations that triggered my fight–freeze–flight so I can manage it in real time. Let me also say, I have not come close to perfection.

To develop your ability to control your behavior, you will need to notice, in a split second, when your mind has strayed from your intention to remain calm and respectful. Ideally, you will develop enough awareness to notice the switch before you act and to say, instead, the more respectful and powerful things that you have practiced. We are so used to responding instantly when someone speaks that we think one second of silence will make us seem slow. Instead, it will make you seem thoughtful, especially if that little moment of time is used to prepare a coherent, measured thought instead of a curt rebuttal.

Even after you make the decision to treat people more respectfully, your brain will still urge you to say disrespectful things to people you do not respect and who you disagree with. Mindfulness is a practice that will significantly increase your ability to be aware of and manage your impulses to be disrespectful and to engage in approaches that, as I mentioned earlier, will make you even more effective than you already are.

The collaboration among science, psychology, social science, and the contemplative traditions has developed the practices of mindfulness and compassion cultivation. These practices can be found in different forms in almost all faith traditions

THE MARTIAL ARTS

As is evidenced by the years of practice required to become a master martial artist, learning to manage your fight–freeze–flight response and developing the leadership skills to create optimal results in imperfect—if not dysfunctional—business and organization environments is not easy. The master martial artist must have incredible commitment. As with the training of our special operations forces, the challenge is to learn to channel your anger and fear in a constructive direction while remaining focused on the task at hand.

Years ago, I attended a martial arts presentation about the concept of blending with force. There are both hard and soft martial arts, just like hard and soft power. Examples of hard martial arts are karate, jiu-jitsu, and taekwondo; their practitioners focus on striking, speed, and power. Aikido, tai chi, and judo are examples of soft martial arts, and they involve redirecting movement, using an attacker's momentum against them, and balance. There is a saying in the soft line of martial arts thinking: "After the storm, the oak is broken, and the willow remains standing."

The instructor, my long-time friend Don Sloane, a licensed

clinical social worker, practices Tai Chi and Buddhist meditation. He explained that when someone attacks him, he does not meet force with force. He demonstrated how he blends with the force directed at him and is then in position to redirect that force. He had members of the audience run at him to knock him down. As they drew near, he stepped out of the way but in alignment with their path. He demonstrated how it takes little energy from him to redirect their pathway down so they fall on the floor.

Don then said that, as they are falling, he has three choices. The first is that he can smash them in the head as they fall. The second is that he can refrain from smashing them in the head ("'Cause I'm a nice guy") and let them fall. The third option is to refrain from smashing them in the head, let them fall but then catch them, putting them gently down and then lightly touching them in vulnerable places to let them know it is not his intention to hurt them, although he could.

He went on to say that his goal is to be so masterful that he can protect the other person from hurting themselves. He pointed out that at a lower level of mastery, his choice to protect himself from harm involves either running away or hurting the other person.

A light bulb went off in my head: When someone attacks me verbally through direct communication or passive-aggressive behavior, the ultimate level of mastery would be to mitigate the damage they are intending while helping them save face. I also realized that I would need to be a master at managing my own fight–freeze–flight response and develop a repertoire of communication scripts and skills to do that.

Becoming a master of the martial arts requires years of practice and patience. The good news is that you can make a "just-enough" change without becoming a master. But it will take some work and some practice. In my experience, working on myself and as an executive coach, simply making the commitment to treat people with respect regardless of how they are behaving will affect how you are experienced by the key stakeholders in your organization. Over the first six months, two to three hours per week of planning and practice will allow you to make a significant positive impact on how others evaluate your behavior. After that, you will probably need one to two hours per week to maintain the advantage you have gained.

CHAPTER 7

MAKING THE COMMITMENT TO CULTIVATE COMPASSION FOR PEOPLE YOUR BRAIN TELLS YOU DON'T DESERVE IT

Buddhist philosophy and meditation practices have made a significant contribution to helping me change the wiring in my brain when it tells me that someone does not deserve respect. In his book *The Art of Happiness*, the Dalai Lama says, "If you want others to be happy practice compassion; and if you want yourself to be happy practice compassion."

Stanford University researchers working with Thupten Jinpa, as well as scientists from other disciplines, have developed compassion cultivation training. Jinpa wrote *A Fearless Heart: How the Courage to Be Compassionate Can Transform Our Lives.* He is a professor at McGill University and chairman of the Mind and Life Institute, which "is dedicated to promoting dialogues and collaborations between the sciences and contemplative knowledge, especially Buddhism." Jinpa has been the translator for the Dalai Lama for close to 30 years.

My colleague and friend, Robert McClure, yet another licensed clinical social worker, was trained to teach compassion cultivation training and certified by the Stanford University Center for Compassion and Altruism Research and Education (CCARE). CCARE was founded by James Doty, professor of neurosurgery at Stanford University, and by His Holiness the Dalai Lama. Combining the ancient wisdom of Tibetan Buddhism and the science of the West, CCARE supports research to understand the impact of compassion and altruism in our lives and trains teachers to provide compassion cultivation training.

At the time, Bob was the manager of the Sharp Healthcare Employee Assistance Program. Sharp, one of the most recognized healthcare systems in the United States, has made the decision to implement a comprehensive compassion cultivation training program for patients, staff, and the public. Shortly after he finished the Stanford program, Bob called to ask if I wanted to be a participant.

I said yes, thinking that, as a person who is a licensed mental health professional, has completed a great deal of psychology and executive coach training, and who has been in therapy myself, I would learn some new techniques. The course was two hours, once per week, for nine weeks. Bob requested a commitment from all participants that we would listen to a 15–25-minute recorded meditation at least five times a week for the remaining eight weeks of the program.

I quickly bought into the definition I learned in class: "*Compassion* is the wish that others not suffer, accompanied by the urge to help end the suffering of others." *Empathy* is the ability to experience enough of other people's feelings to know what they are feeling. (Too much empathy, called *empathic distress*, can be as problematic for interpersonal relationships as too little.)

When you have enough empathy to recognize that someone is suffering or in pain, compassion means that you also have the wish they not suffer and the urge to do something to alleviate that suffering. My understanding is that Buddhist philosophy does not dictate that you should always act on that impulse. Equally important for leadership and management as well as life in general, the concept of compassion does not mean that people should not be held accountable for their actions.

During the fifth week of the program, I was engaged as part of a team of coaches who were working to create a culture change in a large corporation. As often happens during a culture change, the people in the organization start to resist and behave in both abrasive and passive-aggressive ways.

The consultants and coaches also get frustrated and need to manage themselves in order to remain helpful. In fact, managing yourself (referred to as *emotional intelligence* in the popular literature) is a critical competency for successful leaders (business, political, religious, and others), managers, consultants, and executive coaches. Over the years, I have become good at it, although not perfect; I still lose my cool at times. Of course, now as an executive coach, it is much easier to remain dispassionate when not in the trenches on a day-to-day basis with the people and situations that are generating strife.

But in this case, I was strongly triggered and knew that if I acted on the impatient, frustrated, and angry impulses I was experiencing, I would not be effective for my colleagues and clients, and I would certainly not be effective for myself.

That day, I listened to the recorded meditation modules on "Cultivating Compassion for Self" and "Cultivating Compassion for People for Whom It Is Difficult to Have Compassion." After only one hour, I was better able to manage my own reactions and increase my effectiveness in addressing my clients' issues.

Surprisingly, it stuck. After that, I noticed that I had become even more effective in noticing when I am triggered. Despite practicing the meditations infrequently, years later, my ability to notice and manage getting triggered has remained at a much higher level. Also, my ability to, in real time, use the alternative responses I have practiced has increased significantly. I have rewired my brain.

I hope you will stay with me while I take a brief tangent into my personal religious and spiritual philosophy. I am an agnostic, which, to me, means I do not know whether there is or is not a God. While I do not know whether God exists, I find it valuable to consider what God would want from me in a given situation. (If you were to ask this of yourself, you can insert whatever entity works for you—God, the universe, the Force, my family, people I admire, etc.)

This quote circulates periodically on the Internet and is usually (and erroneously) attributed to the Roman Emperor Marcus Aurelius: "Live a good life. If there are gods and they are just, then they will not care how devout you have been but will welcome you based on the virtues you have lived by. If there are gods, but unjust, then you should not want to worship them. If there are no gods, then you will be gone but will have lived a noble life that will live on in the memories of your loved ones. I am not afraid."

Whoever said it, the sentiment is a valid one. Whether you believe in God, gods, or nothing, being committed to adding value to others and treating others with compassion is not a bad way to go, either because of the rewards you will receive in this life or the next.

Making the commitment to cultivate compassion for everyone, including people that my brain tells me do not deserve that compassion, is one of the most important decisions of my life. Once I made the commitment, my ability to manage myself increased significantly. In my experience as an executive coach, once an abrasive executive makes the commitment to cultivate compassion, there is a noticeable change in their life and their impact on others.

I want to restate that cultivating compassion does not mean letting others off the hook for poor performance or inappropriate behavior. Cultivating compassion means developing the awareness that they are in pain and developing the urge to do something to help alleviate that pain. But you can still hold them accountable.

There are several elements to cultivating compassion:

- Calming and focusing the mind
- Cultivating loving-kindness and compassion for yourself and others
- Appreciating shared common humanity
- Actualizing compassion in action

My understanding is that the second point above, cultivating loving-kindness and compassion for yourself and others, involves cognitive (thinking), emotional, and behavioral change. In my experience personally and as a coach, making the commitment to cultivate compassion, even for people your brain is telling you do not deserve it, is critical to accomplishing this or any change. Even if you do not experience feelings of tenderness, warmth, and regret for the suffering of others, the practice can make a significant difference in your ability to manage how you respond.

Below, I have described my experience with compassion cultivation and with meditation in general to give you a better sense of what is involved. I thought about making this a separate chapter in the next section of the book, but I am putting it here to keep it connected with the important context above. More importantly, I am not qualified to teach meditation or compassion cultivation, and I want to be clear that it is not my intention to do so.

My understanding is that brain plasticity is a principle of neuroscience that means that the brain can change and grow from birth to death. "What fires together, wires together" is a phrase that suggests that what we experience, think, feel, and do changes our neural pathways. If you often think about the images and thoughts associated with anger, resentment, and fear, you will reinforce the neural pathways that trigger these reactions within you. And you may build new neural pathways as well.

During compassion cultivation practice, you focus on images and thoughts that reinforce or build new neural pathways to increase their frequency and strength so you increase your ability to recognize suffering or pain in others. You also focus on images and thoughts that strengthen or build neural pathways to increase the frequency and strength of your having the wish that someone not suffer or be in pain and the urge to do something to alleviate that pain.

The compassion cultivation practice that I learned always started with breath awareness to calm the mind. The practice is to keep your focus on your breath, notice when your mind has strayed, and then bring your mind back to focusing on your breath without judgment.

The research studies suggest that each person may require a differing amount of practice to get results. The current thinking is that between 10 and 30 minutes of practice, three to five times per week for eight weeks is required to experience results. Advanced meditators or mindfulness practitioners may focus on their breath, on other sense objects, or on other images for longer periods.

My experience is that 20–30 minutes of practice three to five times per week will make a significant difference in your overall level of calmness and your ability to manage spikes of anxiety, frustration, and anger in real time.

One of the keys to breath awareness, to meditation, and to mindfulness and compassion cultivation, in general, is to notice when your mind wanders and then bring it back without judgment. I have been taught to think something like *There goes my mind. Come on back. Refocus.* I have also been taught to remember where my mind went, because that is often what is causing me the most stress.

Like virtually everyone, I tend to get frustrated and judgmental with myself after my mind wanders several times. I find myself thinking things like, *This won't work; it won't work for me* or *You'll never learn this.* I also think variations of *You aren't smart enough to get this right.*

When I start to judge myself, I have been taught to recognize that judgment and to say to myself something like *Isn't that interesting? Now I am calling myself names.* I might think something like *OK, brain, thanks for sharing. I know you have my best interest at heart. But, you are not correct. I am going to refocus now.* As I do this over and over, I am weakening the neural pathways that drive these thoughts and strengthening the ones that recognize these thoughts and feelings without judgment. I am also increasing my ability to shift to a more positive internal conversation and feelings.

Both positive and negative judgments of yourself are the tip of the iceberg for what are called *mental models.* The mental models causing both negative and positive self-evaluations are wired into your brain's neural pathways. They involve beliefs about what is true, what works, what is valuable, and what is the right thing to do. The mental models triggering negative self-judgment involve a range of things, including questioning what a competent professional (or worthwhile person, for that matter) should be able to do, what you are able to do, why you can't do something, what's wrong with you, etc.

After practicing breath awareness to calm and focus my mind, I then proceed to compassion cultivation practice. In the Stanford approach I learned from Bob, there are several steps. These include cultivating compassion for someone you love and then cultivating compassion for yourself, for someone you don't know well, for someone it is difficult for you to experience compassion for, for a specific group of people, and for all people. (In Buddhism and the Stanford model, this last step is referred to as *cultivating compassion for all sentient beings.*)

Each step has a similar subset of steps. The following steps are paraphrased from the meditation to cultivate self-compassion. This is important because most of us who are identified as abrasive speak to ourselves with a lot of judgment and reprimand. We then project that out onto other people. So developing compassion for yourself is a significant factor in changing our communication style.

The practice below is closely paraphrased from the recording I received from Bob McClure in the Stanford Compassion Cultivation Training program he facilitated. The phrases suggested in the meditation are traditional. Some people find that they do not feel authentic for them. The meditator is encouraged to use phrases that fit for them and are appropriate for the situations and the people they are directing compassion to.

There are several modules. The first module is breath awareness, which is followed by a module on cultivating compassion for a loved one, which I've included. I have closely captured the language from the meditation on cultivating compassion for oneself. There is a period of silence between each of the points to allow you to focus on the image, thoughts, and feelings you are experiencing.

1. Picture someone for whom you feel a great amount of love. Notice the feelings of tenderness and warmth this brings into your heart and how this makes you feel.

2. Now think of a time this person was going through a difficult time. Notice how you feel a sense of concern based on a feeling of tenderness toward your loved one. Notice how you feel for his or her pain and have an urge to reach out and help.

3. Feel with all your heart the wish that your loved one achieves freedom from suffering, and rejoice in the thought of his or her happiness.

4. Imagine yourself as a small child, free and vulnerable, or at an age you can remember from your childhood. Wouldn't you feel protective toward this child? Instead of negative judgment, criticism, and reprimand, wouldn't you relate to this child with tenderness and a natural sense of caring?

5. Let this feeling of tenderness and caring toward this childhood permeate your heart.

6. Now, with these feelings, silently recite these phrases:
- May you be free from suffering.
- May you be free from fear and anxiety.
- May you experience peace and joy.

7. Notice how you feel about yourself when you think of such an experience. How does your heart feel? Do self-critical judgments arise in your mind, making you believe that, at some level, you are no good and that you deserved what you experienced?

8. Now consider whether there are more constructive ways of relating to yourself, especially in the face of suffering and difficulties. Just hold the intention that you really do not want to suffer. Just as when confronted with the suffering of a loved one, you responded with feelings of concern, tenderness, and the urge to do something about it, recognize that you can respond to your own suffering, failures, disappointments, and pain in a similar way, with a sense of nonjudgmental concern, tenderness, and the urge to do something about it.

9. Consider how it would feel if you were to relate to your suffering with a greater degree of acceptance instead of self-pity. Consider how it would feel if you were to relate to yourself with a tenderness and a sense of caring instead of self-incrimination and negative judgment. Consider how it would feel if you were to relate to yourself with more tenderness, warmth, and true acceptance with the thought, *Yes, I am OK.*

10. Now visualize a compassionate image that could represent a source of wisdom, strength, love, and caring for you. This could be the image of a wise person whom you deeply admire and respect, or it could be the image of a light at your heart, or it could be the image of an expansive and deep blue ocean or a firmly rooted tree. If you are a religious person, it could be an icon or symbol that has deep meaning for you. Cultivate this image in your mind. Feel that in the presence of this compassionate image you can be completely yourself. There is no need for pretension. You do not have to be someone other than yourself. There's no judgment, no critical voice of reprimand. Instead, what you find is simple acceptance with warmth and tenderness. Dwell on this feeling of receiving unconditional acceptance.

11. Retain this compassionate image as you breathe. What does this feel like? Then, as you breathe in, visualize warm light rays emerging from your compassionate image, which touch all parts of your body. Imagine that as these light rays touch you. Imagine that they soothe you, ease your suffering, and give you strength and wisdom.

12. As the session draws to a close, let your heart be touched by this feeling of warmth, tenderness, and caring for your own needs, and rest your mind simply on the natural rhythm of your breath.

STEPS TO MAKING

THE CHANGE

CHAPTER 8

MAKE THE
COMMITMENT

The first and most critical step for success at changing anything is to decide that it is the least you can do because it is the right thing to do and that you would do it even if you were experiencing no outside pressure. In this case, we are talking about treating people respectfully even when they are behaving in ways that you think do not deserve respect. Even if you believe this is all PC bullshit, it is still important for you to know the arguments for and against making the commitment so you can more easily manage doing the least you can do. This approach holds people accountable while maintaining respect for them as human beings. Besides being the right thing to do, my nonlegal understanding is that you will also minimize the threat of complaints, grievances, and lawsuits.

So if you are an abrasive executive or even a bully, it is likely that you hold one or more of the following beliefs:

- Nobody told me I am having a negative impact.

- In fact, I am not abrasive. The people who are complaining are oversensitive and weak. They should be able to handle direct communication.

- The people who are complaining deserve my comments and tone, because they are lazy, dishonest, and underperforming.

- I can't believe the company is more concerned about my communication style than they are about the laziness, dishonesty, and underperformance of the people who are complaining.

- There is nothing wrong with how I communicate. This is an example of our overprotective, politically correct society.

- I do not have the time to analyze and rewrite everything I say. I am working too many hours as it is.

I believe there is some truth to all of the perspectives above. We live in a politically correct, overly protective culture, where it may be reasonable to think people shouldn't be so fragile. We might argue that they need to develop the maturity, resilience, and tools to maintain their motivation and sense of well-being in the face of losing, failure, rejection, and even hostility.

Sometimes, I am concerned we are moving toward the world described in Kurt Vonnegut's short story "Harrison Bergeron."

Vonnegut writes that, in the year 2081, amendments to the US Constitution dictate that all Americans are fully equal and not allowed to be smarter, better looking, or more physically able than anyone else. To enforce the equality laws, citizens must wear "handicaps": masks for those who are too beautiful, loud radios that disrupt thoughts inside the ears of intelligent people, and heavy weights for the strong or athletic.

At the same time, one of my core values is to respect all human beings, regardless of whether my brain is telling me they don't deserve that respect. Our special operations forces, the greatest warriors on Earth, believe that part of their commitment is to lead with humility and to protect people who can't protect themselves. All environments contain contradictory values, messages, and sometimes, goals. One of my first mentors, Rick Kinyon, told me that success as a leader requires that I remain productive and drive results, despite the contradictory messages in the environment.

In the current leadership literature, these are referred to as *polarities*. They can also be called *paradoxes* or *dilemmas*. The key point is that these are not problems to be solved. Both sides of the polarity are needed for high performance. Here are some examples of the polarities that exist within any business, organization, or group of human beings:

- Centralized/decentralized
- Directive/empowered
- Reduce cost/improve quality
- Serve the organization/serve the customer
- Serve the team/take care of yourself

Here is my message: Holding people accountable while treating them respectfully as human beings may seem like a polarity or a paradox, but it is not. Both can be done together. Doing only one creates negative results.

So, let's address the potential responses to each of the six beliefs previously mentioned.

NOBODY TOLD ME PEOPLE FEEL DISRESPECTED AND DEMEANED

It is likely that nobody has told you clearly enough how your reactions affect them personally and professionally. The first time you get a direct communication may be when you are removed from your position. In my experience (both personal and as a coach), most abrasive executives need a threat (which I refer to as a metaphorical smack in the head) to decide to change.

If you are the owner of the company, no one is likely to tell you that you need to stop leaving a trail of wounded people behind you. If you are the CEO, you will probably get carefully worded hints or suggestions from your board. If you are not the owner or CEO—and you are lucky—your boss may give you what one of my favorite managers used to call "a dog-dirt-honest communication."

For several reasons, your board, your boss, or human resources are likely to be less clear than you'd like—or than you'd be in your own interactions—about what they think about your behavior and what the consequences may be for continuing. Why? There are several reasons:

- You are very valuable, and they believe that the threat of offending or losing you is greater than the negative impact of your behavior.

- They are conflict avoidant and do not want to have a heated conversation with you, so they talk in generalities and are not clear about wanting a change.

- They have told you how you are perceived and what changes are wanted but have not communicated the consequences, because that is the part of the discussion most likely to create an angry reaction from you.

- They do not know how to handle your potential argument that you are not doing anything wrong: You are—at least in your estimation—appropriately dealing with a bunch of poor performers who are overly sensitive.

- They do not know how to handle the (often true) argument that others are doing the same thing. Why are you being singled out?

- The overall culture of the organization is abrasive, and human resources or the corporate attorney has decided that the expectation for a change in behavior needs to be applied across the board. They may have informed your boss not to act until an organization-wide policy has been announced.

- Especially if you are the owner, people are not likely to tell you that they or others feel disrespected and demeaned by you. As the owner, no one can fire you, but valuable employees can leave, and you can be sued.

If you are the CEO, although no can fire you, you will most likely experience the negative impact of your communication style on morale, productivity, profitability, and potential grievances and lawsuits. Cheryl Dolan and Faith Oliver, writing on HBR.com, pointed out, "Bullies, especially bullying bosses, are unaffordable." Even if you don't lose your job, you will pay the price.

No one may call you on your communication style before it is too late, so it's important to recognize the problem and make the decision to do (at least) the least you can do before you experience these consequences. Doing this has the potential to take your leadership and business results to an even higher level than your warrior spirit alone.

If you are the owner or CEO and you have asked for coaching, I take my hat off to your integrity, courage, wisdom, and humility, as well as your warrior spirit.

I AM NOT ABRASIVE; THE PEOPLE WHO ARE COMPLAINING ARE OVERSENSITIVE AND WEAK

Perceptions are facts. The fact that other people perceive you as abrasive means that you have to act as though it's true, regardless of whether you believe their assessment is inaccurate or based on their own projections, misperceptions, or weakness. Except for some incredibly unusual people (e.g., Steve Jobs), success as a leader and success as a businessperson are related to managing perception.

Executives and leaders are expected to create a high-performance work environment. Holding people accountable is part of that. Acting in a way that others identify as disrespectful (regardless of whether you believe it is) is not only counterproductive but, in our environment, exposes the company to significant liability. The expectation is that you will create a positive work environment whether or not the people you are working with deserve it.

Sales and account management professionals are held accountable for their impact on and success with prospects and clients unless the prospects or clients are grossly out of line or behaving in illegal ways. (And even then, they may be held accountable for results.) Sales and account management people do not keep their jobs if they say, "The prospect or client is wrong. I did not disrespect him" or "The client deserved my response."

So, too, executives and leaders are accountable for the impact they have on others within the company. A big piece of their job is to create a high-performance environment where everyone wants to do their best.

Part of creating this type of environment is hiring the right people. Equally important is creating an environment of both respect and high accountability. As with hard and soft power, one without the other has negative impact.

One last thought: Regardless of right or wrong, executives should be held accountable for acting in ways that might be illegal and might subject their company to lawsuits and other sanctions. According to Robert Sutton's *The No Asshole Rule*, the TCA (total cost of assholes), while difficult to calculate, is very expensive—in time, money, and workplace wellness. For more research to back this up, visit *workplacebullying.org*.

THE PEOPLE WHO ARE COMPLAINING DESERVE MY COMMENTS

The argument against your targets inherently deserving a harsh tone because of laziness, dishonesty, or underperformance goes to your core purpose, your *why*. If you believe in a higher power, is it possible that your higher power put you among all these lazy, dishonest, underperforming people so that you could learn love and forgiveness? Most of the world's traditions and religions say some version of "hate the sin, not the sinner."

If you do not believe in a higher power, does your personal belief system include a value that says all people should be respected as human beings? If you do not have such a value, are you committed enough to being the best, achieving great things, or serving others that you will commit to changing your impact? The research says you will be better able to meet and exceed your goals with a motivated workforce.

I CAN'T BELIEVE THE COMPANY IS MORE CONCERNED ABOUT MY COMMUNICATION STYLE THAN THEY ARE ABOUT UNDERPERFORMANCE

I agree with this sentiment. Most companies tolerate behavior and performance that keep them from being a high-performance organization. There are a number of reasons, including the blind spots and political ambition of leaders, poorly designed performance management systems, and employment laws balanced in favor of the employee.

However, it is what it is. The only thing you control is what you do. I would argue that justifying your own less-than-stellar behavior because other people are doing the same thing is not consistent with a warrior spirit.

THERE IS NOTHING WRONG WITH HOW I COMMUNICATE

Back to the concept of polarities and paradox. You may be making a defensible argument by saying that society is overly protective. However, I hope I have successfully made the argument that both hard and soft power are required for optimal performance.

There are certainly organizational cultures that are so conflict avoidant that even holding people accountable for failure to deliver results or for unprofessional behavior is considered harsh and abrasive. Even if you have been respectful and matter of fact, you can be perceived as doing something wrong if someone gets upset. (I have found that deeply committed nonprofit organizations are more likely to fall into this particular misunderstanding of respect.) In these cases, most reasonable observers (and, from my understanding, employment law attorneys) would agree the executive is appropriately fulfilling their role. The result is that poor performers stay in their positions for years while top performers carry too much of the load or leave.

Keep in mind that this is a polarity. Viktor Frankl and others have made the argument that, no matter how badly someone is treated, they have the choice of how to respond. At the same time, the great leader or executive takes their team and resources to a higher level than most people can imagine. Regardless of who you are working with, you are not a great executive unless you create the conditions where everyone can grow and improve.

I DO NOT HAVE THE TIME TO ANALYZE AND REWRITE EVERYTHING I SAY

It does take work and time to make a change. It does take time to rewire your brain's neural pathways and to assure that people perceive and welcome the changes you are making. But in my experience, it is not as hard and time consuming as you may think.

Because of your time investment, you are likely to generate increased productivity from the people who work with and for you. They will also waste less time complaining about you. They are likely to want to deliver more. Fewer people will try to sabotage you. This means you will be able to accomplish more with less effort, because your team will contribute more. I would guess the ROI of your time investment results in 5–10 times the result in overall productivity and elimination of waste.

In my experience, making the commitment to change how you communicate has a surprisingly positive impact on your ability to do it. After all, you are a warrior. Once you commit to something, you become incredibly effective and productive.

Finally, it is easier than you may think, because you do not need to completely change who you are. This is about managing perception, not about reality. If you do this correctly, you will need to change somewhere between 10% and 15% of your communications. That's it.

CHAPTER 9

TELL PEOPLE WHO YOU ARE AND WHAT YOU STAND FOR

Throughout history, the greatest leaders have told people who they are and what they stand for. They have done this using a combination of stories and purpose statements. Today, purpose statements are referred to as *core purpose statements*, *personal mission statements*, and, most recently, in the words of Simon Sinek, *why* statements.

It is no accident that I began this book with my story about getting fired. Based on what I understand about the neuropsychology of the brain, I am hoping that the story I told in chapter 1 has resulted in you deciding that you:

- Like me

- Trust me

- Believe me

In his book *The 7 Secrets of Neuron Leadership*, my colleague Bill Reed writes about the biology behind influencing and leading people. He says, "According to numerous research studies, including one conducted by the London School of Business and Management, delivering information in a story format increases retention by 1400%. The best story format is the age-old three-act play made famous by Shakespeare. If we apply modern neuroscience, we see that different neurotransmitters and chemicals are stimulated during each act. In act I, whether I'm telling a story to sell a customer or to inspire my team, my goal is to get someone to like me. In doing so, I stimulate dopamine. In act II, my goal is to get them to trust me. To do this, I need to first increase tension to gain attention by stimulating cortisol production. Finally, in act III, I want to increase GABA production, which has a calming effect. I can now get them to logically believe me."

Bill recommends that in act I, you communicate that you have human characteristics similar to or admired by the people who are listening, which will help them like you. In act II, you must alert people to a threat or danger. Warning them both stimulates tension and lets them know you care about their well-being, which encourages trust. In act III, you must demonstrate that you have the knowledge and competence to help them overcome the threat so they believe you.

Here's a meta-example: I wrote in chapter 1 that most abrasive executives have good intentions and that I believe they are not recognized or acknowledged for their warrior spirit. This was to connect with you by communicating that I respect you and that, like you, I have gotten negative feedback about my style. Next, I wanted to alert you to two threats: that there is a danger to your career and that there is an aspect of your leadership and communication styles that keep you from being the best and/or being right, achieving great things, or serving others. Finally, I have attempted to demonstrate enough knowledge and competence that you would respect what I am writing and believe there is value in reading more.

Also in chapter 1, I described a core value: my belief that all people should be respected. Although it was not a fully formed core purpose statement, this realization provided the motivation and direction I would need to get through this challenging period. Because knowing your core purpose is so important to great leadership, I want to tell you the story of how my statement has evolved.

IDENTITY AND PURPOSE

Almost 20 years ago, my colleague Fran Fisher invited me to attend her program "Living Your Vision." Fran is a master certified coach who designed an intensive process to help people identify who they are, what their purpose is, and how to live it. As I flew to Bellevue, Washington, to attend the three-day program, I reminded myself that I needed to muzzle my New York cynicism if I wanted to learn anything.

During the first phase, we were to identify who we are. My understanding is that this comes from a Buddhist tradition to change your name when you achieve enlightenment to express your true self. Walter Meyer tells me that many Native American tribes also adopted a name in adulthood after they achieved some feat. Geronimo got his name after he won a victory on the feast of St. Jerome (*Jeronimo* in Spanish). Children had sort of a temporary name until they chose or earned a permanent one. The Sioux chief Young Man Afraid of His Horses earned his name in battle as well.

We went through a series of exercises to identify situations in our lives that exemplified who we are. We listed times we felt proud, successful, challenged, in the zone, angry, etc. Then we worked with each other to distill the underlying themes that represented our central idea of ourselves. We were to turn these into a statement of who we are and declare it in front of the room.

I was stuck. My situations had several themes but not one or two common ones. Finally, the program leader asked a staff member to work with me privately. (It turns out she was a therapist.) Over a half-day conversation, I realized that I have always been ambivalent. Ambivalence is often interpreted to mean weak feelings. In my case, it meant powerful feelings pulling me in different directions. No wonder I was having difficulty figuring out who I am.

Ultimately, I decided that I am a person pulled strongly in several directions. I also realized that I had become very good at managing this. I came up with the following statement, which I shared with the rest of the participants: "I am the no-bullshit master of paradox and ambivalence."

One of the other men in the class said, "Yeah, right. No bullshit" in a sarcastic tone.

I thought about it and said, "You're right. I do bullshit. But not very much." So I changed the statement to "I am the mostly no-bullshit master of paradox and ambivalence."

Twenty years later, when I am conflicted, I still ask myself, "What would the mostly no-bullshit master of paradox and ambivalence do?" I have a vision of myself on a longboard, surfing a rough ocean of paradox and ambivalence. That image, by itself, creates calmness and focus. Then I find someone I trust and start identifying how I am pulled. In a short time, I have figured out what I am going to do.

The second part of the class was identifying your personal mission. I am sad to say that I did not identify mine by the time the class ended.

After the program ended, Fran asked me to provide business coaching for her director of coaching, Kathy. She wanted me to share the knowledge and approaches I had learned from being the COO of a successful, fast-growing organization.

Kathy and I liked and respected each other, although we had quite different coaching styles. Kathy was trained in the International Coach Federation model, which emphasizes asking powerful questions while "holding a sacred space" for the coaching client to explore themselves and surface their own answers. I had training in the ICF model and respected it. I was, however, more willing to teach models and processes. More importantly, I have a tendency to make direct comments and challenges in ways that Kathy felt were inappropriate for a coach.

During one conversation, I made one of these comments. Kathy stopped and challenged me on what I was doing. I thought about it and said, "I guess I can be provocative."

In an annoyed voice, she asked, "But in the service of what?"

Again, I had to think. Finally, I responded, "In this case, I was intending to provoke growth and healing."

There was dead silence. "Jordan, that is your purpose," she said.

In my provocative style, I responded, "Kathy, who's coaching who?"

This was a powerful moment. Over the next few years, I amended my purpose statement to be "To provoke and support growth and healing." Because I am committed to changing my style, I have learned to ask myself, "What is my purpose?" when my brain is suggesting that I tell someone what a jerk I think they are. After I remember, I ask myself, "What do I need to do to provoke and support growth and healing?" As I said earlier, I am far from perfect, but I am a hell of a lot better at this than I used to be.

After my work in compassion cultivation, I added a purpose statement that supports the primary one: "To cultivate compassion for people my brain is telling me do not deserve it." And my recent work with The Honor Foundation (THF) has created a new understanding about purpose statements. From THF, I learned that special operators receive rigorous training that establishes the conviction that they need to be about *we* and not about *I*. Because of this, they have difficulty, when they transition to the civilian world, describing to interviewers what they did during their service. They also have the challenge of translating their success in incredibly complex and dangerous leadership challenges into civilian language as well.

THF uses Simon Sinek's highly effective model, described in his books *Start with Why* and *Find Your Why*, to help transitioning special operators communicate who they are and what they stand for. I had the privilege of attending *Find Your Why* sessions conducted by THF founder and CEO, Joe Musselman, and THF vice president of programs, Jeff Pottinger.

My current *why* is "I help no-bullshit executives end the complaints and dysfunctional conflict, so their teams do great things."

(To me, it has the same core meaning as my first mission statement, "To provoke and support growth and healing." I have been testing it out, and the response to this new statement is more positive. I anticipate that I will continue to change the language over time.)

Here are some other *why* statements:

"To serve as a leader, live a balanced life, and apply ethical principles to make a significant difference."

—Denise Morrison,
former CEO of Campbell Soup Company

"To act in a manner that brings out the best in me and those important to me, especially when it might be most justifiable to act otherwise."

—Mahatma Gandhi

"To live by the code of the West. My word is my bond, and I ride for the brand."

—Rex Tillerson,
former secretary of state

I realize that Rex Tillerson was part of a controversial administration, and mentioning him may stir up reactions. I included his statement here because it is one of the best I have heard. He explained that *I ride for the brand* refers to the fact that cowboys in the Old West were hired by different ranchers. This is a way of saying that he is loyal to the person he is working for.

THOUGHT LEADER PERSPECTIVES ON THE IMPORTANCE OF PURPOSE

- Ralph Waldo Emerson wrote, "The purpose of life is not to be happy. It is to be useful, to be honorable, to be compassionate, to have it make some difference that you have lived and lived well."

- The German philosopher Friedrich Nietzsche wrote, "To forget one's purpose is the commonest form of stupidity."

- In 1989, Stephen Covey brought the concept of a mission statement into the business world through his best-selling book, *The 7 Habits of Highly Effective People*. As part of his second habit, he recommended that people write their own mission statement in addition to the one for their company.

- In a *Fast Company* article, Stephanie Vozza wrote, "Twenty-five years later, personal mission statements, sometimes called purpose statements, are proving to be a good tool for high achievers."

- In an *Inc.* magazine article, Rhett Power said, "Personal mission statements are an important component of leadership and personal development. They force you to think deeply about your life, clarify its purpose, and identify what is truly important to you. Personal mission statements also force you to clarify and express as briefly as possible your deepest values and aspirations. It imprints your values and purposes in your mind so they become a part of you. Integration of your personal mission statement into your weekly planning is also a way to keep your vision constantly in front of you."

Rhett goes on to give his four reasons having a personal mission statement is important:

- It integrates who you are.
- It provides focus.
- It simplifies any decision-making processes.
- It holds you accountable for your decisions and actions.

THE SINEK MODEL

Simon Sinek has provided one of the most recent and impactful perspectives in the conversation about personal mission or core purpose. Sinek says that all great leaders, whether of companies or movements, communicate in the same way. Sinek calls it the *Golden Circle*.

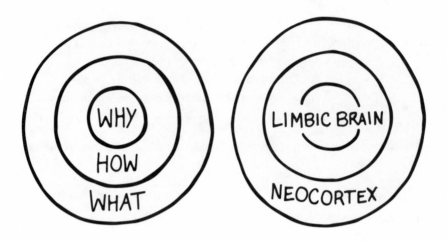

Why

How

What

What is in the outermost circle. Sinek says that "every person and organization on the planet knows *what* they do. Some know *how* . . . *How* is the middle ring. *How* could also be your proprietary process or differentiating value proposition. But few people or organizations know *why* they do what they do."

According to Sinek, your *why* is the innermost circle—the core. Most people work from the outside in: They start with *what*, then move to *how*, and then to *why*. Most are able to move from *what*, the simplest, clearest thing, to *how*, but if they get to *why* at all, they are unclear themselves on what that *why* is, and they have a hard time explaining it to others.

Inspired leaders communicate from the inside out. They start with the *why* and work back to the *what*. This is true of not only businesses, but it is the way Martin Luther King Jr. led his movement. Steve Jobs of Apple, King, and other inspirational leaders start with what they believe in—the *why*. Then they defined *how* they were going to make things into *what*.

Sinek says, "People don't actually buy *what* you do, they buy *why* you do it." As Sinek points out, King said, "I have a dream," not "I have a plan." And he says that this is all grounded in biology—not psychology.

The *Homo sapiens* brain, the newest part of the brain, corresponds to the *what* and is the center of rational thought and language. The inner two sections make up our limbic brains, the more basic instincts: emotion, arousal, and memories. This includes trust and loyalty, which are key to attracting competent people who are willing to follow you.

The *why* is responsible for behavior and decision-making, but it has no capacity for language. Communicating from the outside in can send lots of information via language, but if you want to inspire behavior—get people to make decisions—you have to start from the inside ring and work outward.

Often, gut decisions don't seem rational and can't be easily explained to others, but that is because they are not coming from the part of the brain (the *what* circle) that is rational and has a clear vocabulary. Even with all the facts, it just doesn't "feel" right. (This is often why it is hard to get people to change political opinions. They are more interested in how a candidate or issue makes them *feel* than any words or facts or figures that contradict that feeling.)

Appealing to the way people feel matters. People will work for you for less money if they believe in what you believe in. If they are just there for the paycheck, that loyalty can be bought by someone with a larger paycheck. A "rational" person will take a new job that gives them more money and a bigger title, but they will stay in a job where they are appreciated, like what they are doing, and *feel* like they are making a difference. As a leader, you need to believe that what you are doing makes a difference in the world, and you need to get others to believe that as well so they will follow you.

Should you decide to identify your *why*, there are several approaches. Simon Sinek's model in *Find Your Why* is a great place to start. He wrote, "Press your memory for the stories that have made the biggest difference in your life. Some occasions you recall may be momentous, but many won't be. What's important is the *quality* of the memory, the specific details you remember and the strong emotion you feel as you tell the story to someone else. Because it is very difficult to see the golden thread that connects our stories, we suggest . . . that you work with a partner or with a facilitator, respectively."

Below are my current *why*, *how*, and *what*.

- *Why*: "I help no-bullshit executives end the complaints and dysfunctional conflict, so their teams do great things."

- *How*: "First, I spot the elephant in the room (what is not being seen or addressed). Then I speak plainly and directly about that elephant with compassion and respect. The next step is to reach alignment and commitment on what we must do and how we must show up to be successful. The last step is to unleash growth and change."

- *What*: "I draw on the knowledge, expertise, and wisdom within my client and within my clients' team. I directly challenge blind spots with compassion. My unwillingness to hide from the truth is a source of strength for others. I introduce alternative perspectives, processes, and skills. I also introduce lean and agile methodology to address business issues that have root causes in the business systems and processes. I find deep satisfaction in working with people I care about and respect. I am at my best when fighting for a principle or cause."

In summary, great inspirational leadership is rooted in who you are and what you stand for. Most leaders do not know what these are for them. If you want to be an inspirational, effective leader, developing your personal mission, core purpose, or *why* statement should be considered the least you can do.

CHAPTER 10

CONDUCT YOUR RESEARCH

G reat leadership involves many things. These include vision, strategy, planning, driving for results, creating change, and—of course—managing yourself. There is also an important aspect of great leadership that involves managing or perhaps influencing perception. But whether you are interested in taking your leadership to the next level or simply protecting yourself, you must determine what you need to do to achieve great results.

As we discussed earlier, it is likely that everyone in the value chain of your organization has information you do not have. Therefore, learning what you do not know is critical. You also need to create the perception that you have done what should be done to achieve great results. You need to conduct research to determine both. And they are not the same thing.

This second type of research, managing or influencing the perception of others, has two elements. The first is to understand the perceptions held by your key stakeholders about you and your leadership and communication style. These stakeholders include your peers, your reports, and your internal and external customers. It might be helpful to think of your key stakeholders as your internal market and imagining that you are doing market research. It does not matter whether they are correctly reading your intentions or interpreting your behavior. You simply need to know what they think.

The second element is understanding yourself. This is because you do not control the perceptions, judgments, or behavior of other people. The only thing you control is yourself. So the only leverage you have to create the change you want is to change how you act and react. Therefore, you need to understand how your brain is wired to take in and process information and make decisions. You also need to know your deepest values, assumptions, preferences, and blind spots.

Over the years, I have spoken with many executives who were surprised that the behavior that got them acknowledged and rewarded in one company was criticized and punished in another. The same is true in different parts of the country or the world. Among New Yorkers, I tend to be perceived as having lost my edge. In California and the Midwest, I am perceived as overly direct, if not tactless.

In order to determine the actual perceptions of you that are held by your stakeholders, you have three main research options available. In most cases, you will want to use at least two of them.

360 ASSESSMENTS

360 assessments collect what are referred to as *observer ratings* of your leadership behavior among superiors, peers, reports, and other groups you might select. The assessments list somewhere between 30 and 170 leadership behaviors and ask your network (your market) to rate how often they perceive those behaviors in you. In most assessments, your raters are able to make specific comments, which can bring increased clarity to the numerical ratings.

Most organizations that provide these assessments survey between 8 and 20 of your key stakeholders to capture a snapshot of your leadership strengths and to determine areas for development. This provides you, often, with access to previously unknown information about what your internal market perceives and what they want from you. Many executives who use these assessments are surprised to find that areas they think are weaknesses are perceived as strengths and vice versa.

The ratings from reports, peers, and groups such as customers are typically anonymous, but those of your boss and superiors may be identified. Anonymity and confidentiality are important factors affecting the validity of the information you get from the assessment. Your raters may be concerned that you will retaliate if you find out how they rated you and what comments they made. This is managed by reporting the rating of peers and reports only if three or more responded.

You may be concerned that others within the organization will see the ratings and comments. This can be managed by using an outside party who commits to providing the report of results only to you. In most cases, the issues around anonymity and confidentiality are well managed, whether they are handled within the organization or by an outside party.

INTERVIEWS CONDUCTED BY A THIRD PARTY

Direct interviews generate more personal and nuanced information from your stakeholders than a 360 assessment. Most stakeholders are willing to give honest feedback to an objective third party who promises anonymity. This type of interview is often conducted, with your permission, by an executive coach.

Whether the interviewer is a trusted internal person or an outside party, they should interview your boss and then meet with you and your boss together. The purpose of the private discussion is to give your boss the opportunity to think through what they want to say to you. The job of the interviewer or coach is to support your boss to clearly communicate what they see as your strengths, opportunities, and development areas.

It is especially important that they clearly tell you about anything that could threaten your career. This is critical to create a fair process for you, your boss, and your company or organization. For several reasons, your boss may not have been as completely clear and direct in previous conversations. I have had many of these meetings over the years. In almost all of them, the executive heard something that they had never heard before.

In addition to interviewing your boss, the interviewer or coach will conduct as few as 6 and as many as 20 interviews, each lasting between 30 minutes and an hour. The results from all the interviews should be presented in random order to protect anonymity; the trust of the interviewees is a critical factor.

The two questions in the simplest interview are *What are (your name)'s strengths as a leader?* and *What are (your name)'s challenges and areas for development?*

The interview might include additional questions as well, such as these:

- How would you describe (your name)'s relationship with peers?

- How would you describe (your name)'s relationship with reports?

- What does (your name) do that inspires you to improve, innovate, and drive for excellence?

- What does (your name) do that discourages you, confuses you, or disengages you?

- What is the one thing (your name) should change that would make the most difference to the quality of your work and the quality of your work life?

- What is the one thing (your name) should change to be more effective as an executive for (your company)?

INTERVIEWS THAT YOU CONDUCT

There are two types of interviews you can conduct yourself.

The first type is intended to uncover the same information gathered in the aforementioned third-party interviews. These are exceptionally difficult to do yourself. Your reports and peers are likely to be hesitant to tell you the truth because of fear of retaliation or because they do not feel comfortable giving negative feedback. Even your superiors may hesitate to give honest feedback for fear of angering you, discouraging you, or hurting your feelings.

The other reason it is difficult to conduct these interviews yourself is that you, the interviewer, must not react to what is said if you want to get good information. I recommend that you will get much better information if a third party conducts these interviews privately.

FEEDFORWARD

There is a second type of interview or conversation that is very important for you to have. This is called *feedforward*. The feedforward process was developed by Marshall Goldsmith, one of the most recognized and respected executive coaches in the world. Marshall explains that feedback gives you information about what people perceive are your strengths and areas for development based on what you did in the past. It may also provide information on what actions and behavior your stakeholders (your internal market) believe will create success in the future. *Feedforward*, on the other hand, focuses on what actions and behaviors your stakeholders want to see from you in the future. One advantage of this is providing options you may not have considered. Another advantage is finding out what will help you create alignment and buy-in.

Feedforward creates an implied agreement that the people providing the feedforward will change their perception of you if you demonstrate (at least some of) the suggested actions or behaviors. This is critical, because without an implied agreement, you may make significant changes that are not noticed or that are noticed but not valued in terms of changing perception.

To give you a good feel for the core of the feedforward process, I want to describe how Marshall introduces the concept during his talks. He asks his audience to think of a goal they have. Then he sets up a competition. The person who has asked the most other people for input on their goal wins a prize.

The instruction is to have a very brief (two- to three-minute) conversation with other people at the talk. The participants are asked to tell each other their goal without revealing any background information—for instance, "I want to build collaborative relationships with my team. Do you have any suggestions?" Marshall's process focuses on getting information on what you as an executive want to change about your leadership and communication style. Depending on the situation, executives I have worked with have sometimes asked questions more related to business and organizational processes and culture—for instance, "I want to cut turnover in my department. What can I do to be successful?"

The participants are usually surprised by the quality of information they get from strangers who know nothing about their background or the context of their challenge or problem. I certainly was.

When conducting feedforward interviews, your job is to jot down everything that is said, without commenting. The only thing you can say is "thank you." You are not allowed to agree, disagree, or otherwise evaluate the input. Almost always, you will receive suggestions that you have not thought of before.

Remember: Everyone in your organization and in your value chain knows something you don't. Generating perspectives and options is incredibly important when managing complex, rapidly changing environments. Increasingly, great business and other organization leaders need to have a continuous inflow of perspectives and options to be successful.

HOW TO APPLY FEEDFORWARD

As was mentioned above, data about what your stakeholders want and do not want from you is key to managing or influencing perception. In addition to providing much of this data, feedforward is one of the most powerful techniques for changing how you are perceived. The fact that you have the humility and courage to engage in feedforward interviews will significantly change how people perceive you and open the door to more productive relationships.

So how does feedforward work? Here's how I use feedforward myself and with my executive coaching clients. You do not need an executive coach to practice feedforward. Marshall recommends that everyone practice this method to get options on how to improve their results.

Your first step is to request a brief (15–30-minute) meeting with your key stakeholders, such as your boss, superiors, peers, and customers. Executives wanting to change the perception that they are abrasive or even bullies would be advised to also have these conversations with family and friends.

You might begin by saying, "I have gotten feedback that people experience me as disrespectful. Some people have said they have experienced me as damaging to them. If you are one of those people, I want to apologize. My goal is to build respectful relationships that contribute to positive business results. Do you think I am working on the right thing?"

(A quick note: The apology is critical for most others to let go of their negative assessment if they have experienced you as demeaning, disrespectful, and certainly, damaging to them. Unless you are one of the few people who can convince others that you mean something when you do not, you need to find something you genuinely believe you should apologize for.)

You would then listen to and take notes on whatever they say. You cannot disagree with them. If they say you should be working on something other than the goal you stated, write it down. You can ask questions to get a clearer take on what they mean, but do not argue with their opinion or offer alternative perspectives.

If they agree that you are working on the right goal, you would then ask something like, "What would you like to see me do or say in the future for which you would rate me as excellent in this area?" They are then likely to tell you what you should have said or done differently in the past. In my experience, this is a difficult point in the process, because you will be very tempted to "straighten them out" about what was really going on and why you did or said exactly the right thing. Instead of disagreeing, it is effective to ask something like, "What could I have said that would have been more effective?"

If you would not be breaking confidentiality or providing information that is not appropriate to give, you could say something like, "Would it be OK if I give you some background information on that situation so I can hear how you might have approached it differently than I did?" Essentially, you are asking for coaching. This is very powerful in terms of demonstrating your humility, courage, and intention to change. Right off the bat, a percentage of your stakeholders will shift their perception of you. These conversations will increase most of your stakeholders' willingness to help and their willingness to tolerate your human imperfections.

As I mentioned before, these conversations are a very informal negotiation. Essentially, you are establishing an unstated agreement that your stakeholders will change their perception and ratings of you if you make some behavioral changes. Without these conversations, you could change a lot, and your changes might never be noticed.

You are trying to change perception, not reality. Your request for feedforward is a form of market research. If you truly intend to change, you need to determine what your market wants you to do or say. Your intentions are not enough.

Think of it as going to a foreign country and learning to speak their language. If you continue to speak your primary language, no one will understand your intention. You do not have to actually do or say the things your stakeholders are identifying. But you do have to know what they are so you can make informed decisions and have increased control over the impact you are having if you do choose to do the least you can do in either sense of the phrase.

Feedforward usually does not work if you do not believe that changing is the right thing to do. People will read your tone and nonverbal cues and know you don't mean it. Few people possess the extraordinary acting skills required to get others to believe they are sincere when they are not. And if you are the type of person this book is written for, I am pretty sure you are not one of them.

After your first round of interviews, you will typically meet with your coach to review what you heard, look for trends, and identify the key issues. If you are not working with a coach, you can do this yourself or with someone you trust and respect. I strongly recommend you have at least one other person review your interpretation of your feedforward responses and ask for their perspectives and suggestions.

Your initial goals may or may not change. Often, the goal stays the same, but it is restated so that it clearly reflects the input you received. When I coach, I strongly recommend a meeting with you and your boss (or your board chair) to be sure you are aligned with them on the final articulation of your goal.

Then you would do a second round of conversations, starting with, "I received a lot of input about what my goal should be and what people would like to see me say and do going forward. I have reviewed it and put together a goal with behaviors I will demonstrate and wanted to let you know what I am working on." You could also ask, "Given the changes in the goal, may I ask again what you would like me to say or do in order to achieve this goal at the highest level?" You might also ask a select number of people to give you periodic ratings and more feedforward.

You can also ask people you trust if they would be willing to give you a "stop" signal if you are exhibiting ineffective behavior in a meeting or other public situation. These could include patting a cheek or pulling an ear.

SELF-ASSESSMENT

Self-assessments are time- and cost-efficient tools, often used in executive coaching, to help you better understand yourself. This understanding will allow you to know your assets and strengths so that you can leverage them. You will also learn about your weaknesses and areas for growth, so you can anticipate your reactions and manage those as well.

The people who create the most accepted assessments typically have a PhD in psychology or a related behavioral science. You can choose from assessments that provide information on your personality style and your communication style. Other self-assessments will provide information on your leadership and management competencies, your preferences for taking in information, problem solving, decision making, and interpersonal relationships. The reports of your results will usually tell you your likely strengths and weaknesses related to the area the assessment measures.

With few exceptions, your responses to the questions on a self-assessment are compared to a population of other people who have taken the assessment. In some cases, this might be a specific group of people, such as successful executives in corporations. In other cases, your scores are compared to a general population. To determine the value of the information for you, it is important to know how the population is constituted. This might include such things as age ranges, genders, work status, educational status, countries of residence, and primary language.

There are no perfect assessments in terms of the validity of the concepts in the assessment and the accuracy of the scores you receive. Psychometricians may disagree with practitioners about whether certain assessments are valid enough to be used. In my opinion, there are two reasons to take a widely used self-assessment: To learn the model and to learn how the assessment rates you.

Regardless of your own score, understanding the model will provide valuable information. For instance, the Influence Style Indicator postulates five strategies that can be used for influencing people: rationalizing, asserting, negotiating, inspiring, and bridging. Regardless of your scores, just learning the model can provide you with previously unknown options for gaining buy-in and mitigating behavior that is identified as abrasive.

Learning how the assessment rates your strengths and challenges on the area being measured is also crucial. For instance, you might learn that an assessment rates you high on dominance and low on empathy compared to how other people responded. Because the ratings of any assessment have what is referred to as an *error of measurement*, you then need to determine whether the information fits and, if not, what is the accurate rating. Most people need a coach or consultant to help them do this.

There are four reasons that you might not think the information you get from a self-assessment is accurate. First, you may not understand how to respond to the questions because they were asked in a language other than your own. Or, due to your culture and education, you may have interpreted the question differently than the test designers intended. Another possibility is that you were having an unusual day in terms of stress, the amount of social interaction you were having, or some other factor that influenced you.

You also might not understand the meaning of the concept being tested. For instance, one of the categories in the Myers-Briggs Type Indicator (MBTI) is judging–perceiving. Most people interpret the word *judging* as meaning "criticizing" or "belittling." As used in the MBTI, the term refers to whether or not you are systematic, scheduled, and methodical and whether you plan or start early.

You may have answered the assessment based on what you truly believe about yourself, but you may not have accurately assessed yourself. For years, I tested as an ENTP on the Myers–Briggs (extrovert–intuitive–thinker–perceiver). After taking an in-depth seminar, I realized that I had been answering the questions as my father and uncle would answer them. Although I have taken the Myers–Briggs several times and never tested this way, I am sure that I am, in fact, an ESFP (extrovert–sensor–feeler–perceiver). My master coach is in agreement.

Finally, the score you received may not be accurate. As I mentioned, all assessments have an error of measurement. There are no assessments that are scientifically valid enough to be 100% accurate. Therefore, it is important that you take the responsibility to determine whether what you are being told resonates. In most cases, it is recommended that you review the assessment with someone who is trained to review it with you.

CHAPTER 11

ANALYZE YOUR DATA, ESTABLISH GOALS, AND IDENTIFY ACTIONS

Because you have read this far, I assume that you have decided you want to change the perceptions others have of you. Another way of saying this is that you have decided to change the impact you are having on others. You may believe this is the right thing to do, or you may want to do the least you can do to protect yourself and your job. Either way, your next step is to analyze the data from your research to identify goals. Then you need to develop a plan of action to make the changes in perception you want to achieve.

ANALYZING YOUR STRENGTHS AND WEAKNESSES

As I mentioned earlier, self-assessments give you information about yourself so you can leverage your strengths and manage your weaknesses. Below are several examples of information you might get from self-assessments.

You might learn from the Influence Style Inventory that your primary approach for influencing others is to make strong rational arguments followed by asserting your authority. You might also learn that you spend little time on other influence styles, such as inspiring, negotiating, or bridging. If your market research suggests that people experience you as demeaning, you might increase your use of these other styles in business discussions.

From the Myers–Briggs, I discovered that, as an extrovert, my brain is wired to think out loud. People who think out loud do not fully know what they are thinking or feeling until they hear themselves say it. In my case, this proclivity resulted in my saying things that were unnecessarily harsh. It also resulted in my colleagues thinking I was shooting from the hip.

The primary technique I use for managing my need to think out loud is to review with trusted advisors the conversations I intend to have that involve negative feedback. When asked a question about complex issues, I might frame my initial response by saying something like, "That is a complex issue. Is it OK if I think out loud?" If you are an introvert, you process information internally. Rather than thinking without responding, it might be helpful to say, "The response to your question is complex. I need to think a bit."

After losing my job, my outplacement counselor gave me the California Psychological Inventory (CPI) 260, a world-class instrument used for both hiring and executive development. I learned some critical information that helped me identify aspects of my personality that contributed to my getting fired.

The CPI 260 uses your responses to 260 questions to provide scores on 26 different measures that are grouped into several categories: dealing with others, self-management, motivations and thinking style, personal characteristics, and work-related measures. My responses were similar to the most effective executives in the world on 23 of the 26 measures. My scores were significantly lower on three competencies in the self-management group: responsibility, self-control, and good impression. In my case, my counselor and I agreed a low score in responsibility did not mean I made promises and did not keep them; it meant that I was less likely than successful senior executives to fulfill job requirements that I did not think were worthwhile. In my case, a measured lack of self-control meant that I was less likely than the most successful executives to be diplomatic rather than direct. The low good impression score meant that I did not care whether I created a good impression as much as the most successful executives.

My outplacement counselor circled these three scores and said, "There is your derailment." While I had heard all this before, seeing my responses scored against successful executives was powerful. This understanding motivated me to develop alternative ways of responding to the situations that triggered these responses.

ANALYZING THE DATA FROM YOUR MARKET RESEARCH

The data from your 360 assessment, third-party interviews, your own interviews, and feedforward provides information that can be analyzed and then grouped into general categories and then into specific competencies. This is a complex process. Luckily, some good resources are available to help you.

Two of my favorite resources are *Compass* by the Center for Creative Leadership, and *FYI for Your Improvement* by Lombardo and Eichinger. There are a number of strong leadership models as well. These include *The Extraordinary Leader* by Zenger and Folkman; *The Servant Leader* by Ken Blanchard and Phil Hodges; and *The Leadership Challenge* by Kouzes and Posner.

To give you a sense of what is available, I have adapted some of the competence categories from these sources below. I have included a broad range, so you can do a quick self-assessment of your strengths and developmental opportunities. This will help you assess what other competencies you need on your team. It will also shed light on whether the frustration and anger you experience with others might be related to deficits in your own competencies and skills. Review them to see where you think you might need to focus.

STRATEGIC THINKING AND PLANNING

The strategic thinking and planning category describes how you understand your industry, market, and the politics, economics, technology, or other areas that might impact your market in the future. It also depicts how your vision, mission, goals, and strategy may need to change, given your assumptions about what will occur in the future. This category can help you design an understandable strategic plan that inspires buy-in and continuously communicates the strategic plan so everyone incorporates the plan into their decision-making processes. Finally, this category indicates how you'll create an environment where everyone is motivated to scan for and identify developments that challenge the assumptions behind the plan and the strategies for implementing it. You will implement a process that enables everyone to identify challenges to the plan, evaluate those challenges, and adjust the plan.

BUSINESS ACUMEN

Business acumen is your knowledge and ability to institute an effective business model, create accurate financial projections, and plan and manage your business. It also includes your understanding of the market.

LEADERSHIP COMPETENCIES

Two recognized models of leadership competencies are Direction–Alignment–Commitment (from the Center for Creative Leadership) and Character–Interpersonal Skills–Personal Capability–Focus on Results–Leading Organizational Change (from Zenger and Folkman's *The Extraordinary Leader*).

ORGANIZATIONAL COMPETENCIES

These include your ability to establish: commitment to the mission and team above personal interest; innovation, creativity, and high performance; a value chain that identifies everyone's role in producing value for the customer; production systems that promote quality, productivity, and efficiency; continuous improvement; and to manage rapid change when necessary.

MANAGEMENT SYSTEMS

Management systems include your ability to establish effective systems for production, service delivery, management, internal and external communication, communications, results or performance, accountability, staff development, and recognition.

MANAGEMENT AND INTERPERSONAL SKILLS

An abbreviated list of management and interpersonal skills includes accountability, building and maintaining relationships, oral and written communication, conflict management, decision making, delegating, developing (coaching) others, directing, driving results, empowerment, giving negative feedback, negotiation, performance management, planning, problem solving, and team leadership.

MANAGING YOURSELF

Also known as emotional intelligence, managing yourself includes how well you know and communicate who you are and what you stand for, integrity, accountability, managing strong emotional reactions and maintaining composure, maintaining motivation and focus, resilience, and your work–life balance.

DEVELOPING GOALS

Laura Crawshaw, one of the most recognized experts on abrasive workplace behavior, says that behavior is always a response to a threat. This threat may involve losing or not being the best, not achieving great things, or not serving. Therefore, leaders and abrasive executives need at least one goal related to changing the way they respond to whatever the threat is for them. This goal will usually fall into the managing yourself category.

They will usually need a second and sometimes a third goal related to improving their leadership or management skills so they can better address the issues causing their threat reactions. Sometimes, they need a goal related to improving the business model, strategic plan, or the production systems.

You will be more successful if you focus on what you want to create rather than what you want to eliminate. Goals are most effective if they are positive—for instance, "communicate respectfully" rather than "decrease disrespectful communication." You want the people who will evaluate your change to be focusing on the new behavior rather than the old behavior.

You will increase your success rate if you frame your goals in language that demonstrates you heard the feedback from your 360 assessment and from the interviews of your key stakeholders. The objective is to have them feel that you heard them. If your feedback said that you do not delegate, "improve delegation" is likely to be more impactful than something more general like "improve productivity."

There are two types of measures: objective and subjective. The measures for goals related to behavior that is identified as abrasive are largely subjective: the ongoing ratings of your stakeholders.

Professional and personal development is an ongoing journey, not a finite process. A real example appears in appendix C. It has been edited to protect confidentiality.

CHAPTER 12

CHANGE YOUR MENTAL MODELS

I n 1990, Peter Senge said, "Mental models are deeply ingrained assumptions, generalizations, or even pictures and images that influence how we understand the world and how we take action."

Our mental models drive (or cause) our behavior. They include what we think is true, not what is actually true. They include what we must do to get results, given what we think is true. Mental models also include what we believe to be the right thing to do from a practical, ethical, and moral perspective.

Mental models are similar to but not the same as what they

represent. We don't need to focus on our mental models until we want to create change. Individuals, teams, organizations, and cultures have mental models. Shifting or changing mental models is the most powerful way to change behavior and sustain that change.

If you are acting or reacting in ways that get you identified as abrasive or as a bully, your actions and communications are driven by your mental models. Laura Crawshaw said that abrasive behavior is triggered by a threat; the threat creates anxiety, and anxiety creates a response. In other words, something happens (a stimulus) that triggers anxiety in you. That anxiety triggers a defensive response. This may be a sarcastic tone of voice, or you may say something that is identified as disrespectful or demeaning. To change your (semiconscious) interpretation that something is a threat, you need to change your mental models related to that event.

Let's do a quick example. Quickly, without thinking, what is your first impression about who is the executive in each of the following pictures—or is anyone in the picture an executive?

Do you notice the assumptions you have about executives that drive this first impression? Are executives men or women? Are they older or younger? Are they working on the project or on the side observing and directing? What race are they? What is their body language? Would they be talking or listening? Did you notice there are no people dressed like construction workers or wearing Hawaiian shirts?

Mental models are composed of two elements, a *paradigm* and a *philosophy*. As I reviewed the various definitions and descriptions of these elements, I found that there is a lot of overlap between them. Their definitions often contain elements of the others. Understanding that they are imperfect, I have provided definitions with less overlap to clarify the elements of a mental model and what it takes to shift or change it.

PARADIGM

A *paradigm* is a model, pattern, or example. It is a widely accepted example belief or concept. For our purposes, it is important to remember that there are no perfect paradigms. Each is a representation of reality. Therefore, your paradigms are models, patterns, or examples that you believe to be true. Below are examples of paradigms:

- The creation of the universe
- The Earth is round
- Social systems (capitalism, socialism, etc.)
- Successful companies
- The inherent nature of people

- Quality systems
- The role of management
- Leadership
- Empowerment

If you are trying to change behavior that is identified as abrasive, you will have an individualized combination of the above paradigms that drive how you react to whatever is happening. You will also have many other paradigms not mentioned above.

For instance, you might be a believer, an atheist, or an agnostic who believes that people are inherently self-serving or well meaning and generous. Whichever you believe will influence the mental model you have about effective leadership and management. Your paradigms interact with each other to create a unique set of assumptions and beliefs about the universe and everything in it.

PHILOSOPHY

The term *philosophy* can mean several things:

- The study of ideas about knowledge, truth, the nature and meaning of life, etc.

- A particular set of ideas about knowledge, truth, the nature and meaning of life, etc.

- A set of ideas about how to do something or how to live

I am using this third definition: your beliefs about how you should live your life. In my paradigm about mental models, the philosophy element requires that you ask yourself three questions, and your answers will be influenced by your paradigms:

- What do I need to do to achieve the results I want?

- Is this worth doing?

- Do the actions I must take meet my moral and ethical standards?

The following are examples of the mental models involved when you have a frustrated or angry response to a report or peers who got poor results on a project. Ask yourself these questions:

- What do I believe is the impact on the following?
    - The client
    - Profitability
    - Morale
    - The reputation of my team
    - My reputation
    - My evaluation of myself

Your response will also be driven by your assessment (mental model) about

- What is poor performance versus a flawed part of the design process

- Who or what is responsible for the poor results

- What must be done to fix it permanently

Here is a real example of how mental models impact behavior. To minimize emotional reactions that might get in the way of understanding, I am using an issue that is different from yours. In fact, it is the reverse.

I have coached many executives who are not identified as abrasive. Rather, they are identified as conflict avoidant or even "too nice." Typically, they receive coaching because they need to improve their ability to provide negative feedback and hold people accountable in a timely manner. They avoid telling their reports that their performance or behavior does not meet expectations and will result in consequences. Often, the performance or behavioral issues have gone on for months or even years. This has had an impact on quality, productivity, and morale. High performers resent it and may try to leave. Such an executive often spends a lot of time in conversations with these problem performers—usually, much more time than with their high performers.

In my experience, there is a central, powerful mental model driving these executives to delay telling someone that their performance or behavior does not meet expectations and will result in negative consequences for them. The mental model underlying their lack of action is that this clear and direct communication is harsh and potentially damaging. They do not want to bring out a cannon to shoo a housefly.

My job is to help executives shift or change their mental models and the underlying paradigms and philosophies that create them. Whether it is a coach or someone else, most people need a trusted, objective person to act as a sounding board, to challenge their assumptions, and to suggest alternative ways to view things.

Remember Jim from the introduction, who was backing toward a cliff? I suggested two things you could say to him.

One possibility would be to say, "Jim, stop stepping backward, you idiot. There's a cliff behind you. Don't you check where you are going?" Obviously, this is done with a critical tone, even reprimanding.

A second possibility would be to interrupt and say, "Jim, if you keep stepping backward, you may fall off the cliff." This would be done with an urgent, direct tone with the intention of alerting him to take action to avoid hurting himself.

There is a different paradigm and philosophy behind each. The paradigm might have something to do with how people are motivated and how they learn. The philosophy might be about what is the proper role for a friend or colleague to alert a friend or to report potential danger.

Your mental model determines how you will tell reports that their performance and behavior is not acceptable and will lead to lowered annual increases, bonuses, or perhaps discipline and termination. If someone is performing in a way that will lead to career death, shouldn't you warn them of the danger?

If your mental model drives you to do this with the good faith intention to alert them to what they need to do, you avoid the unintended negative impact of speaking in a way they experience as demeaning. The impact is even greater because they cannot dismiss you as an asshole.

In summary, you need to change—or, at least, shift—your mental models in order to change how you react to events that trigger the frustration and anger that then drives what you do that gets you identified as abrasive.

CHAPTER 13

POWERFUL LISTENING

L istening is the first of two parts of communication. Since no one says exactly what they mean and since people attach different meanings to the same words, listening involves decoding the words that come out of someone else's mouth in combination with their body language when they speak. What you hear and understand is, in large part, determined by what you are listening *for*. And what you are listening for is determined by your mental models.

In case it is not obvious, all leadership and management—good, bad, and mediocre—occurs through communication. Communication is the process by which two or more humans interpret what each other means and intends, which drives how they act in relationship to each other and to a goal. Especially for teams in complex environments that contain opportunities and threats, success is determined by several things that are mediated by communication:

- Shared purpose
- Alignment on mission, vision, goals, strategies, and tactics
- Acceptance of norms (the rules of the road)
- Mutual understanding of models, processes, and skills
- Development, implementation, and improvement of systems and procedures
- Marketing and sales
- Innovation
- Problem identification and remediation
- Directing
- Teaching and coaching

To keep this relatively simple, I have included a classic, linear model of communication by David Berlo.

The S-M-C-R Model of Communication

S ource	Encodes	M essage		C hannel	Decodes	R eceiver
Communication Skills		Content		Hearing		Communication Skills
Attitudes		Elements		Seeing		Attitudes
Knowledge		Treatment		Touching		Knowledge
Social System		Structure		Smelling		Social System
Culture		Code		Tasting		Culture

From *The Process of Communication (El proceso de la comunicación)* by David Berlo. Copyright © 1960. Published by International Thomson Publishing.

Listening is a critical part of communication and, therefore, of leadership and management. Your success at listening is ultimately determined by whether you can accurately decode the message that someone is sending so you understand the real meaning behind their words. If you and the speaker, who encoded the message, agree on what the message is, you have accurately heard and the speaker has accurately communicated. The evaluation and agreement on whether communication occurred may be nonverbal. You may not discuss the meaning of the communication directly but act on the meaning. If you are comfortable with the actions you both take following the communication, you have nonverbally agreed on the communication.

If the speaker is not aware of their mental model, thoughts, and emotions, their words and nonverbals will not communicate their true meaning and intention. Or the speaker may not have the skills to effectively encode their message. And, of course, the speaker may be intentionally misleading. In these cases, the measure of successful listening is harder to determine because people's actions are not consistent with what each expects from decoding the other's message.

Accurate listening is determined by your ability to decode the message you are receiving through words, tone, and body language in a specific culture and context. For a receiver of that message, some of the most obvious blocks to decoding its true meaning include being raised in different countries or different parts of the same country, having different religious upbringing and beliefs (mental models), speaking a different language, or growing up or currently living in vastly different socioeconomic conditions.

BLOCKS TO LISTENING

Differences between the backgrounds and training of the sender and receiver of a message create blocks to listening. People with 20–30 years of experience in the corporate world are likely to encode their messages quite differently than people with the same amount of experience in a family business, a privately held entrepreneurial business, a nonprofit organization, or the military.

There are deeper examples of potential blocks to listening caused by differences in each person's core purpose, or *why*. If the speaker is motivated by serving others and the listener is motivated by being number one, there will likely be aspects of the message that cannot be properly decoded.

Other factors related to accurate decoding involve the wiring of the listener's brain versus the wiring of the speaker's brain. The Myers–Briggs identifies four dichotomies related to how people are energized, how they take in and process information, and how they make decisions. Our awareness of the dichotomies and where we fall on each affects our effectiveness in communicating.

The first dichotomy is introversion–extroversion (I and E). Extroverts process information externally. They need to hear themselves say something to truly know what they think, feel, and intend. Often, the first things out of their mouth are not their ultimate meaning. Their first responses may be experienced as harsh or unclear. Introverts often think extroverts are shooting from the hip, not clear thinkers, or overly harsh in their responses. Introverts process information internally. There is a longer gap between question and response. Extroverts often think introverts are unprepared, don't understand the question, or are trying to be politically correct (or to mislead) in their response.

The second Myers–Briggs dichotomy involves how you take in information. Sensors (S) analyze the data much longer than intuitors (N), who quickly move from a few data points to (correct or incorrect) identification of higher-level patterns and conclusions. Sensing and intuiting have nothing to do with intelligence, but sensors and intuitors may judge and mishear someone who processes information differently than they do.

The third Myers–Briggs dichotomy involves your basis for making decisions. Thinkers (T) make decisions based on logic and reason. Feelers (F) make decisions based on the impact on relationships.

The fourth Myers–Briggs dichotomy is about whether your brain is wired to quickly develop plans and schedules or to "hang loose" and make decisions as things evolve. This is the judging–perceiving (J and P) polarity.

Your training regarding what is and is not relevant greatly impacts your ability to listen. I continually meet executives in technology or financial firms whose decision processes rely on data, and they dismiss the relevance of information about the impact on their relationships and the feelings of those affected by the decision. At the same time, I meet executives whose decision process gives more weight to how people feel than I would. Both extremes create unintended negative consequences.

TECHNIQUES FOR LISTENING

As I mentioned above, one of the measures of successful listening is whether the speaker believes you heard and understood them based on how they understand the meaning of your words and actions in response to their message. There are several techniques you can use to increase the likelihood that you will ultimately hear (i.e., correctly decode) the speaker's real meaning.

ACTIVE LISTENING

Most communication training teaches a technique called *active listening*. The Center for Creative Leadership teaches that you can listen for three things that are stated or inferred by the speaker:

- The facts
- The speaker's feelings
- The speaker's values

While the facts are important and cannot be ignored, listening for and reflecting the speaker's feelings and values will, in most cases, be more effective in understanding the speaker's intention and meaning. Leaders who listen only for the facts have a greater likelihood of being experienced as uncaring or abrasive.

Depending on what you are listening for, you may derive a very different meaning about what the speaker intended to say. So the second part of active listening is to paraphrase what the speaker said and engage in a back-and-forth conversation to reach mutual understanding. When listeners focus on and paraphrase their understanding of why the facts or story are important to the speaker (the speaker's feelings and values), the speaker much more frequently rates the listener as accurate. I recommend that you explore attending a class on these classic behavioral techniques.

EXPAND WHAT YOU LISTEN FOR

You cannot listen neutrally. Your listening is always influenced by your mental models, your intentions, and your knowledge and skills.

Your intention is what you are trying to accomplish in a particular interaction. For instance, if you are trying to fix a problem, you will listen differently than if you are trying to mentor someone. If you are trying to improve morale, you will listen differently than if you are trying to challenge someone or a group to be focused on results.

The more you are aware of and manage your internal conversation, the more likely you are to be an accurate and effective listener. Your internal conversation is both conscious and unconscious. It includes your core purpose—your *why*—and your motivations, assumptions, beliefs, knowledge, skills, and biases.

Since it is impossible to listen neutrally, you can improve your listening by considering what you want to be listening for. Review this partial (but long) list of the things that any leader or executive might listen for when approached by someone wanting to provide a briefing or requesting input or assistance. Identify the ones you are most likely to listen for. Identify those you might want to add. Find out what the people you respect are listening for. "Find out what other respected people are listening for." Add ten additional possibilities or variations to the list.

- Why is this person communicating?
- What does this person want or need?
- Is there a problem? If so, what?
- What are the strengths of this person?
- What is admirable about this person?
- How can I get this person to agree?
- How can I best be of service?

- What is the right thing to do?

- What is a win?

- What is a win for all of us?

- Is there a threat?

- Is there an opportunity?

- Is there data that challenges our assumptions, goals, or strategies?

- Did I contribute to this problem?

- Is there evidence I am right?

- Are there any symptoms of broader systems issues?

- Does anything challenge previous conclusions?

- Is there evidence of incompetence?

- What other perspectives might be possible?

- What are they not saying?

- How do I maintain the upper hand?

Regardless of what you are listening for, your impact can be positive or negative. Much of what determines the reaction of the other person is how they decode your purpose and intention from the questions you ask, the things you say, your tone, and your body language. Their reaction is likely to be positive the more committed you are to make a positive difference beyond your own interests—in other words, if you are committed to a core purpose or *why* that is about making things better, adding value, achieving, or serving, rather than solely meeting your own goals.

MANAGE YOURSELF

Before an important meeting or conversation, do a few minutes of breathing to calm your mind and your fight–freeze–flight reactions. Then ask yourself the following questions:

- Do I actually care about the topic of this conversation or meeting?
- If not, what intrinsic motivation do I have to listen?
- Do I care about the person or people I will be meeting with?
- If not, what motivation do I have to treat them respectfully and try to add value?
- What should be my role in this meeting, conversation, or in general?
  - Give direction.
  - Create alignment.
  - Build commitment.
  - Add value.
  - Hold others accountable.
  - Uncover incompetence.
  - Coach or mentor.
  - Create consensus.
  - Build on strengths.
- How do I manage my judgments, impatience, and annoyance?
- What will I commit to listening for?

CHAPTER 14

SPEAKING POWERFULLY WITHOUT DAMAGING RELATIONSHIPS

S peaking powerfully without damaging relationships is a methodology for telling the truth while minimizing the probability that people will react negatively enough to create long-term damage. It is much easier to tell the truth and maintain a positive relationship when you agree with the other person or people. The challenge for most leaders is to tell the truth and maintain a positive relationship when they disagree.

Expressing disagreement, pointing out other perspectives, identifying the negative impact of what someone did, or directing someone to take an action that is different from what they intend to do is referred to as *negative feedback*. Your ability to give negative feedback while maintaining trusting, positive relationships is one of the most critical factors for your leadership success. You are likely to be successful giving negative feedback if you have a genuine intention to be respectful; use a positive frame for your message; and use the direct, clear, nonjudgmental language described. (Oh yeah, you also have to be credible in terms of your knowledge and expertise as well.)

Unless you are an incredibly good actor or you are completely comfortable saying things that are not true, it is almost impossible to communicate something that is not consistent with what you believe, feel, and intend. If you have read this far, I think the odds are good that you are not someone who can comfortably and convincingly say things that are not true. Therefore, mastering the skill of communicating the truth, your negative feedback, is the key.

As I mentioned in the last chapter, nobody controls how another person will hear (decode) and react to what they say. You have the opportunity to control only what you say and how you say it. Ultimately, each person you speak to determines how they respond, regardless of how positive and respectful you are. Their *why*, mental models, intention, and background determine the message they hear (decode) and how they react.

Therefore, there are no guarantees that you will be successful giving negative feedback while maintaining a positive relationship with any person you give that feedback to. If they are committed to reacting with outrage, anger, or hurt feelings, they will do so even if you are perfect in your delivery.

PREPARATION

The preparation phase of speaking powerfully without damaging relationships is adapted from Tom Crane's book *The Heart of Coaching*. Tom is a speaker, author, and consultant on establishing a coaching culture in organizations.

For me, the key recommendation in Tom's process is to express your positive intention before giving negative feedback. Tom's process includes recognizing that a conversation needs to happen and committing to a date for having the conversation. He also recommends that the date be no longer than 72 hours away.

You must be able to communicate the impact of the other person's actions in a clear manner, without insult or abuse, which will only dilute your message. Therefore, Tom suggests that you practice saying what you are thinking and feeling with someone you trust. This is critical. If you are introverted or do not have someone you can trust, you should at least write out your honest thoughts and feelings. It is very effective to do both.

Most people believe their uncensored thoughts, feelings, and judgments about the person who will be receiving their negative feedback is inappropriate for the workplace and not consistent with their personal values. Because of this, they construct a sanitized version. This version is usually too general and does not accurately convey the critical issues about the behavior, impact, and consequences they want to communicate.

In my personal and professional experience, the unvarnished, uncensored conversation in your head has gold underneath it. I have found that saying and analyzing my inappropriate, unacceptable thoughts and judgments is often critical to constructing a respectful, clear communication. In most cases, no-bullshit executives and just about everyone else are angry and judgmental because they believe the other person has had a negative impact on important goals, principles, or values.

I recommend mining the unacceptable conversation in your head with a trusted colleague in order to get precise and clear about your positive intention and about the behavior and impact of the person who will receive the feedback.

The research says that somewhere between 70% and 95% of what is heard when you speak is determined by your tone and body language, not the words you say. A videoconference introduces a certain distance between speakers, and those nonverbal cues can be more difficult to interpret. On the telephone, a listener has input on tone, but the absence of body language can greatly hamper communication. Written communication has no body language or spoken tone of voice, so there is even greater chance for misunderstanding. These nonverbal behaviors are a crucial tool of conversation. Therefore, a piece of the work with your colleague is to identify and modify the ways you are communicating that will create a negative impact or present an inaccurate communication.

Your tone and body language are determined by your *why*, your mental models, your intention, your communication skills, and your ability to manage your emotions. This is true for almost everyone but the few people who can appear honest when saying things that are not true. To be effective, you must identify an authentic positive intention. This is usually the reverse of what you are angry, upset, or judgmental about. Most people cannot create an authentic communication if they try to clean up their internal disrespectful, inappropriate, or politically incorrect conversation without exploring it.

I routinely ask my partners and colleagues to provide a safe, confidential, nonjudgmental space for me to state the uncensored conversation in my head and to analyze the facts and mental models triggering that conversation.

Then, they help me identify my positive intentions for the person who will receive my communication, as well as for the organization and others involved in the situation. If I do not have a positive intention, they challenge me to develop one by reminding me of what I have previously described as my *why* and my core values. I do this because I know that I must communicate clearly and precisely without insult or abuse, which will only dilute my message and create unintended negative consequences.

Finally, they help me construct a clear feedback statement. I use the Situation–Behavior–Impact (SBI) formula developed by the Center for Creative Leadership (CCL). The formula involves making a brief statement (I try for 15–30 seconds) that describes the situation in which the behavior occurred, a nonjudgmental "behavioral" description of what the person said or did, and the impact on others and the team and organization.

The SBI formula is deceptively simple. In my experience it is one of the most powerful communication tools I have encountered. It can take between 20 minutes to an hour to develop enough perspective to manage myself and to design and practice my positive intention and SBI. In complex situations with important outcomes, it can take a much longer time.

THE TWO PARTS OF COMMUNICATION

Please stay with me while I take a brief tangent into the concepts about communication models I would be willing to bet are new to you. In their book *Pragmatics of Human Communication*, Watzlawick, Bavelas, and Jackson offer several important axioms about communication. One of these axioms is that all communication has two aspects: content and relationship. The content is whatever it is you are talking about—simple enough.

The relationship is more complex: Jay Haley, in *Strategies of Psychotherapy*, says that communication can be "roughly classified into behavior which defines a relationship as *symmetrical* and behavior which defines a relationship as *complementary*." He says that in a symmetrical relationship, "Each person will initiate action, criticize the other, offer advice, and so on." In a complementary relationship, "One gives and the other receives, one teaches and the other learns." The symmetrical relationship can be thought of as equal and the complementary to one up/one down relationships. Most relationships change throughout an interaction, from topic to topic and minute to minute. Depending on the culture, a change from symmetrical to complementary may be determined by such things as rank within the organization, licenses or academic degrees, recognized expertise, and previous success or failure. There are three status possibilities on any topic within a conversation.

ONE UP / ONE DOWN

Participant A
I am superior to you on this topic.
"You are in service to me"

Participant B
I am inferior to you on this topic.
"I am in service to you"

ONE DOWN / ONE UP

Participant B
I am superior to you on this topic.
"You are in service to me"

Participant A
I am inferior to you on this topic.
"I am in service to you"

EQUAL

Participant A
We are equal to each other.
"We are in service to each other"

Participant B
We are equal to each other.
"We are in service to each other"

In many situations, leveraging the one down, "I am in service to you" position is deceptively powerful. You may be in service to someone because they are a client, superior, or peer. In some cases, leveraging the one down, "I am in service to you position" with someone of lower rank is very effective.

The most effective way to leverage the one-down position is to use words that put an "I'm in service to you" frame around what you are going to say. However, the tone of voice should almost always be confident, equal, or even superior in the sense of more knowledgeable, more expertise, etc.

The following are some more examples of how to convey your positive intention and frame your feedback (positive or negative) from the "I am in service to you" position. A key concept is to ask permission before giving information or making well-meaning but unsolicited suggestions.

- I wouldn't be doing my job as your (consultant, coach, service provider, team member, employee, boss, friend) if I didn't:
  - Point out some possible downsides I can see
  - Challenge you on that point
  - Provide another perspective to consider
- Do you want to hear it?

- I want to be as helpful as possible, and the way I think I can be most helpful right now would be to explain:
  - How your agreement works
  - The company's policy on this

- ○ My understanding of the government's regulations
- Is that OK?

- I want to be helpful, but I am not sure what the issue is. Is it OK if I ask you some questions to clarify what has happened and what you need?
- I am interested in supporting your career success. I wouldn't be doing my job as your manager if I didn't give you some feedback about:
  - ○ What you said in the meeting
  - ○ The decision you made about _____
  - ○ The complaint I got about _____
- I'd like to have a conversation about how:
  - ○ We can provide great (improve) customer service
  - ○ We can improve productivity (quality)
  - ○ We can decrease cost
  - ○ We can have a great relationship with other departments
  - ○ You can enhance your effectiveness
- Do you have a few minutes?

FOUR TYPES OF FEEDBACK

Following framing your communication, you need to provide clear information about the situation in which the behavior occurred, and specificity about both the behavior itself and the impact of the behavior.

For instance, you might tell a report who masterfully handled an angry client, "You did a great job today."

That is not as clear and specific as saying, "I overheard your conversation with the angry client you were talking to on the phone this morning. You listened and summarized what you heard them say. You asked for clarification of what they were trying to accomplish and stood your ground on our policy. You asked permission to suggest alternatives. I thought your tone was respectful, composed, and patient. The client called to let us know she felt well served. I am very pleased as well."

If the feedback was more negative, you'd say something like this: "Today, you called in and said you could not make our staff meeting, and you have missed the last four meetings. You recently missed the deadline on your project. The team has commented on your absence from staff meetings, and I am concerned about you but also about your performance."

Wayne Hart, PhD, is a senior fellow with the Center for Creative Leadership, one of the most recognized providers of leadership development and executive coaching in the world. Wayne wrote *Feedback in Performance Reviews* about how to give both positive and negative feedback.

In the book, Wayne describes four types of feedback. Three of them share something in common; they are authoritative. The fourth is quite different; it is informative and empowering. The CCL model for doing this is called Situation–Behavior–Impact, or SBI.

- *Directive* feedback tells the feedback receiver what to do.
  It is literally a "Do this. Don't do this" statement.

- *Contingency* feedback notifies the receiver about a future consequence. It is an *if–then* statement.

- *Attribution* feedback describes the receiver, the receiver's behavior, or the receiver's output in terms of a quality or some other label.

- *Impact* feedback describes the situation in which the receiver acted, the behaviors and statements exhibited by the receiver, and the observable impact on others.

The three types of authoritative feedback are communicated from the position of a one up / one down relationship, at least in the moment. The feedback giver assumes the authority of knowing what should be done (in the case of directive feedback), knowing what outcome will result (in the case of contingency feedback), or knowing how to judge the quality or nature of something (in the case of attribution feedback).

DIRECTIVE FEEDBACK

Directive feedback is appropriate and most effective when urgent action needs to be taken and there is no time for discussion—for example, "We are up against a deadline. Stop gathering data, and summarize conclusions from what you have." It is useful when you have made a decision and want to end the discussion: "Management has decided to go with plan B. Take care of your assignments now." Also, it is welcomed by the receiver who just wants clear direction about what to do—for example, "The highest priority is making a list of prospects. Do that first." In order to maintain a positive relationship, it may be helpful to soften a directive by adding something like, "Please, do that first" or "We need to stop gathering data and summarize the conclusions from what we have."

CONTINGENCY FEEDBACK

Contingency feedback is a form of authoritative feedback that is communicated from a one up / one down position and always contains a clear or implied directive.

This type of feedback informs people about your perception of the potential positive or negative consequences of their performance or behavior. The first part of contingency feedback describes an actual or potential behavior. The second part describes a likely outcome.

Contingency feedback to communicate the possible beneficial consequence for taking actions can be an effective way of directing or coaching, depending on your intention—for example, "If you work on this taskforce, you will get increased visibility among senior management." This can be part of delivering a directive or engaging in a coaching conversation where the receiver has a choice about what action they will take.

Contingency feedback is critical when you need to alert someone that their performance or behavior may lead to a negative consequence. Remember Jim on the cliff?

An example of an early-stage contingency statement about performance and behavior would be, "If you continue to miss deadlines (or get complaints), it will have a negative impact on your career." Later, you may need to be very direct—for example, "If you can't meet your deadlines, I will have no choice but to replace you."

In terms of maintaining a positive relationship, it helps when contingency feedback is preceded by a positive intention: "I wouldn't be doing my job supporting you if I did not let you know that, if you can't meet deadlines, I will have to replace you."

I am not suggesting that you always soften contingency feedback. Especially when you have had several discussions of performance or behavior issues, you may need to be very direct. There are legal and policy issues as well, so it is a good idea to check with your human resources and legal consultants when the situation gets to this stage.

ATTRIBUTION FEEDBACK

Attribution feedback, labeling the receiver or the receiver's behavior, may be the most common of the four forms of feedback. We often do it without even thinking much about it. "Good job," "You took your eye off the ball," or the indirect version, "What were you thinking?" are all versions of attribution. It can be quite effective when delivered with a positive intention to support or coach someone who is open to your input. It is also effective when alerting someone to how they are being judged.

IMPACT FEEDBACK

Impact feedback is offered from an equal position with the intention of stimulating reflection and conversation (i.e., coaching). Whether you are a leader, manager, supervisor, or consultant, there are times when giving authoritative feedback is necessary. I cannot imagine that you can do your job without it. However, authoritative feedback is less likely to trigger reflection and development. It is more likely to trigger a defensive or negative reaction than impact feedback.

When giving impact feedback, it is often more effective to approach a conversation from an "in service to you," or an equal position. This is true when you want to encourage independent thinking or to develop people rather than direct them. It is also true when you are trying to create alignment with equals or superiors.

Impact feedback is more likely to trigger self-reflection, arouse curiosity, and establish the importance of an issue in order to create an opening for discussion and coaching. It takes the feedback receiver out of the spotlight. Instead, attention is focused on the consequences of what the receiver did, without judgment. It informs the receiver about the effect of their actions on other people, the client, the organization, or the executive. Rather than telling the receiver what to do, giving a warning, or judging what the receiver did, impact feedback informs the receiver about how the effects of behavior ripple across the environment.

Impact feedback is more likely to stimulate the receiver to think rather than react to a directive or judgment. Typically, the motivated and engaged receiver of well-delivered impact feedback will want to know more or want to do something to create a better impact that is more consistent with their intention.

In a business setting, I tend to recommend that the impact feedback is most effective when it first focuses on the impact on clients, the organization, and the team. In some cases, it may be appropriate to add the impact on you, personally. When using impact feedback to describe the impact on you, it is often effective to use an "I" statement, such as "I am concerned," "I am frustrated," or "I am pleased."

You'll find a chart comparing examples of impact feedback with the authoritative forms of feedback in appendix D.

Which form of feedback is best depends on the situation. Ask yourself, "Do I want to direct or promote compliance at the risk of triggering resistance, or do I want to promote engagement and commitment at the risk that the receiver will be slow to figure out what to do differently?"

The following are examples using the "in-service-to-you" frame and either an SBI, a contingency, or a hybrid of the two. The examples also include a closing question or statement that I have added to the model.

- **Positive intention:** I want to let you know what I heard about your presentation (said to a peer or subordinate).

- **Situation:** Today, in the meeting, you presented the team's proposed changes to the plan for the fourth quarter.

- **Behavior:** Your presentation was well organized, you spoke clearly, and you handled several challenging questions.

- **Impact:** You held everyone's attention, and our proposed changes were accepted. The CEO told me she is impressed, and I got several other positive comments.

- Recommended but optional break for reflection and response.

- **Closing question or statement:** I want to thank you for your contribution.

- **Positive intention:** (To a subordinate) I wouldn't be doing my job as director and also supporting your success in the company if I did not give you some feedback. Do you have a minute?

  "No."

  "When are you available? We need to have this conversation before the end of the day."

  "OK, let's do it now."

- **Situation:** When you came into the meeting late this morning, I was talking with the VP of sales, the COO, and a potential customer.

- **Behavior:** You sat down, saying, "Sorry I'm late," and started talking about an idea the customer had already said would not work.

- **Impact:** The customer rolled her eyes and later said she does not want to work with you. The COO asked me if I had had a discussion with you about being late. The impact on me is concern about our relationship with this customer, my credibility with the COO, and frankly, a loss of trust in you.

- **Contingency:** This is going to result in a written warning.

- Recommended but optional break for reflection and response.

- **Closing question or statement:** Is there something I am missing?

- **Positive intention:** (To a peer) Jim, I want to be your ally, and I am in a bind.

- **Situation:** Last week, you said that you would have the report for me by today.

- **Behavior:** Today, you told me it will not be done until next week.

- **Impact–contingency hybrid:** Our boss expects this project to be done by this Friday, and I cannot do it without this report. I do not want to complain about you, and I don't want to take responsibility for being late on the project.

- Recommended but optional break for reflection and response.

- **Closing question or statement:** Do you have any suggestions about how to handle this?

- **Positive intention:** (To a subordinate and maybe a peer) I need to have a conversation with you about how we can provide excellent internal customer service.

- **Situation:** I heard from Christine that you and she had a conversation earlier today and that she made a special request from our team.

- **Behavior:** You told Christine that we can deliver, even though the request is outside the company policy.

- **Impact:** Christine later found out that she cannot get what she wants under the existing budget. She is not happy. I am wondering whether you don't know the policy or whether you were avoiding a difficult conversation.

- Recommended but optional break for reflection and response.
- **Closing question or statement:** Is my concern unreasonable?

VARIATION

- **Positive intention:** (Said to a superior or peer) I want to serve you, and I need your help.
- **Situation:** You have asked me to deliver on your project by tomorrow. I am here to serve you and want to follow through on your request.
- **Behavior:** N/A
- **Contingency:** If I do that, I will not deliver on commitments I made to (peer or superior).
- **Closing question or statement:** Would you come with me to talk to (peer or superior) to see if we can work out a change in schedule?

THE POWER OF INTENTION

A quick note about the power of intention, especially in conflict situations: In any interaction, the person who is more committed to their intention will influence the other. For example, you may be about to address an organizational issue with a peer in another function. Let's say that you are committed to a positive, respectful, win–win interaction, and the person you will be talking to is committed to a negative, blaming, win–lose interaction. If you are more committed to win–win than your peer is committed to win–lose, you will take the wind out of your peer's sails by the time the conversation is over. You will not transform your peer into someone who values win–win outcomes, but you will both know that you won.

On the other hand, if your peer is more committed to a win–lose outcome than you are to win–win, you will both know that your peer won. You will probably not exhibit as much negativity and blaming as your peer would, but you might roll your eyes, speak with a negative tone and body language, or say something sarcastic.

If you and your peer are equally committed to your intentions, the result is a stalemate. You both walk away knowing that you did not move the other person from their commitment.

A FINAL THOUGHT

In many ways, the success of your leadership is determined by your ability to give powerful but respectful and compassionate negative feedback. Managing your mindset and your intention is the biggest challenge. They are key to whether, over time, people like you, trust you, and respect you.

CHAPTER 15

HOW TO DO THE LEAST YOU CAN DO—LITERALLY

There is no way that I or anyone else can tell you the literal least you can do to protect yourself from the unintended negative consequences of your leadership and communication style in your environment. Every company and organization has its own culture and underlying rules of communication. Added to that, each company or organization is in a country, state, city, or municipality that has its own unique culture and expectations for how people treat each other as well. Finally, the people in each company or organization have unique backgrounds, personalities, and expectations.

If you are simply interested in protecting yourself, you must determine what you need to do in your company or organization to make sure you are not crossing the line (or to stop crossing the line) that would trigger negative consequences for you. And you must do this in a way that your key stakeholders notice, so they recognize the leadership and communication style changes you have made. Equally important, they must be willing to change their assessment or judgment of you when you demonstrate those changes.

Throughout the book, I have discussed many of the mental models, competencies, and skills that drive leadership and communication style. I have also discussed how to conduct research to determine whether there are threats to you and your career that generate from your style or from anything else.

If you are concerned, you at least need to do enough research to make an assessment of your status. In her book *Taming the Abrasive Manager: How to End Unnecessary Roughness in the Workplace*, Laura Crawshaw presents a set of recommendations, which appear in the next few sections. They are a wonderful summary of most of what appears in this book.

LAURA CRAWSHAW'S RECOMMENDATIONS

Get as Much Feedback as You Can as Soon as You Can

Make it easy (in other words, nonthreatening) for others to give you feedback. Tell them you are concerned that you may be coming across in ways that you do not intend, and reassure them you will be grateful for their frank input. Listen calmly, take notes, ask questions for clarification, but above all *do not attempt to defend yourself.* The goal is to collect data on how you are perceived, period.

Apologize

"I see now that when I interrupt, it might give the impression that I think my thoughts are more valuable. I don't mean to give that impression, and I'm sorry that I did."

As I mentioned before, an apology is necessary if you want people who believe that you have disrespected, demeaned, or otherwise hurt them to change their assessment or judgment of you. Ultimately, it is the judgments of others that determine your level of threat.

At this point you should clarify and ask what behavior they want to see from you in the future. This comes from the feedforward process.

Ask for Further Feedback

"If you see me doing that again, will you let me know? I'd appreciate it."

Thank coworkers for having the courage to open up, and reassure them they are helping—not harming—you.

"Thanks again for speaking frankly. It really helped. It opened my eyes."

continued

Get Help if You Are Unable to Change Your Abrasive Behavior

Ask your employer to refer you to a specialist who works with abrasive individuals, and if that's not an option, seek help on your own.[5]

Laura's last point is important because most people cannot make a change like this on their own. Whether you want to do the literal least you can do or more, having an outside, objective sounding board and thinking partner is likely to be critical.

Hopefully, you have a basic sense of the potential steps you can take to achieve whatever change you decide is right to make.

Whatever your next step is, I want to remind you
that you can draw on your warrior spirit to handle
whatever comes at you.

THANK YOU!

---

5   Laura Crawshaw, *Taming the Abrasive Manager: How to End Unnecessary Roughness in the Workplace.* 2007

SELF-TEST:
ARE YOU ABRASIVE?

This self-test appears in Laura Crawshaw's book *Taming the Abrasive Manager: How to End Unnecessary Roughness in the Workplace.* Laura is the founder of The Boss Whispering Institute, which conducts research and training in the specialty practice of coaching abrasive leaders.

1. Have you ever been asked to:

    a. Improve your communication skills?

    b. Control your temper?

c. Learn to get along with others?

d. Not get so "worked up"?

e. Not be so hard on coworkers?

2. Have you been passed over for promotion and can't get anyone to give you specific reasons for the decision?

3. Have you been passed over for promotion because of your people management skills?

4. Do you find yourself in intense and unresolved confrontations with:

    a. Superiors?

    b. Peers?

    c. Subordinates?

    d. Human resource staff?

5. Have complaints been brought against you for inappropriate conduct, such as:

    a. Harassment?

    b. Discrimination?

    c. Hostile treatment?

6. Do you have a nickname that refers to dangerous behaviors (such as "Axe-Man," "Terminator," "The Ripper,") or dangerous animals ("Pit Bull," "Wildebeest," "Tyrannosaurus")?

7. Do people avoid you at work?

8. Do employees attempt to transfer out of your department or avoid transferring into it?

9. Do you have enemies at work? If so, how many?

10. Do you frequently find yourself intensely frustrated by coworkers?

11. Do you generally feel that you are smarter than your coworkers?

12. Do people choose their words carefully so as not to offend you?

13. Have you received low scores for team building, participative management, or other so-called soft skills on a management skills assessment?

14. Do you dislike coworkers who are less competent than you?

15. Do you take pleasure in demonstrating to others that they are less competent?

16. If so, do you openly refer to selected coworkers as:
    a. Lazy?
    b. Stupid?
    c. Incompetent?
    d. A bunch of idiots?
    e. Other pejorative descriptions?

17. Do you engage in any of the following behaviors at work?
    a. Publicly criticizing others?
    b. Hostile humor or teasing?
    c. Shouting?
    d. Profanity?
    e. Making threats?
    f. Publicly humiliating others?
    g. Temper outbursts?

h. Physical intimidation (such as throwing objects or slamming doors)?

i. Ignoring others or giving others the silent treatment?

j. Name-calling?

k. Making condescending statements?

l. Nonverbal expressions of disdain (rolling eyeballs, snorting, snickering, and so on)?

SCORING

- If you answered yes to any of the following questions, there is a good chance that you are perceived as abrasive: 2, 3, 7, 9, 10, 11, 12, 13, 14.

- If you answered yes to any of the remaining questions, you are behaving abrasively: 1, 4, 5, 6, 8, 15, 16, 17. These questions refer to unacceptable workplace behavior or extreme coworker reactions, signaling abrasion.[6]

---

6   Laura Crawshaw, *Taming the Abrasive Manager: How to End Unnecessary Roughness in the Workplace.* 2007.

THE SEVEN STEPS
OF A FULL APOLOGY

n his book *The Respectful Leader*, my colleague Gregg Ward provides this formula for offering a full apology for behavior that was disrespectful:

1. **Admit it.** Admit, specifically, what you did or said and that you know it was disrespectful. "I specifically said/did XYZ, and it was disrespectful."

2. **Describe how it hurt them.** "What I said/did hurt you and others because it . . . "

3. **Make no excuses.** "I make no excuses for what I did/said; there are no excuses."

4. **Apologize sincerely; ask for forgiveness.** "I sincerely apologize for what I have done and how I've hurt you and others. I ask for your forgiveness." (Then, even if they don't forgive you . . .)

5. **Promise: Never again.** "I promise to never do/say anything like this to you or others again."

6. **Offer to make amends.** Offer to make amends, and ask for permission to make it right. "I would like to make amends for what I've done, and I would like to ask your permission to make it right. Here's specifically what I plan to do to make this right . . . "

7. **Start immediately.** Even if they refuse to give you permission to make it up to them personally, go ahead and start doing the "right" thing with them and everywhere else in your life. You may get permission in the future.

Being the imperfect human being that I am, I had the opportunity to use this formula in the last year. One piece I find particularly challenging is the promise: never again. This is challenging for me for two reasons. The first is that I know I slip up. *Never again* is quite a commitment. The second reason is that, as a person who gets triggered to say provocative things, I know there will be moments when I do not feel committed to refrain from saying what I am thinking the way I am thinking it. Because honor and truth are important to me, making this promise is no small commitment.

Example: Professional Development Goal

GOAL: INCREASE COMPOSURE AND BUILD RESPECTFUL RELATIONSHIPS

MEASURES OF SUCCESS

- Subjective: Improvement in feedback or ratings from reports and peers
- Objective: Achieve promotion

ACTIONS

1. Conduct research (or have my coach conduct research) to identify what leadership and communication style behavior I need to change.

2. Send thank-you email to all 360 raters and people who were interviewed by my coach (if appropriate) by (date). Tell them I will be letting them know my goal when formalized.

3. Discuss with my boss to achieve alignment on the goal and approach by (date).

4. Engage in feedforward with 16 key stakeholders to solicit direct feedback on my goal and desired behavior by (date).

5. Develop a log of situations that trigger my abrasive behavior.

6. Review log to identify the underlying threats and mental models.

7. Identify alternative ways to perceive the threat and alternative responses to the threat.

8. Practice relaxation or mindfulness three to five times per week.

9. Read *HBR's 10 Must Reads on Managing Yourself.*

10. Read the Center for Creative Leadership's short publications on how to give feedback.

11. Read *Taming Your Gremlin.*

12. Find a trusted advisor to coach me on giving negative feedback in a way that is experienced as composed and respectful.

13. Identify two to three colleagues who are willing to signal me when I am displaying behavior I want to change.

14. Conduct quarterly check-ins with stakeholders to determine my progress.

RESOURCES REQUIRED

- Personal commitment
- Support of key stakeholders
- Articles and how-to materials
- Support from a trusted advisor or executive coach

OBSTACLES

- Time—my plate is full
- Resentment for having to do this
- Stakeholders so angry they may not support change

PLAN TO OVERCOME OBSTACLES

- Schedule reading, meetings, and phone calls
- Request input and mentoring from the VP who exhibits respectful but powerful communication
- Discuss with my coach
- Delegate two projects

BENEFIT TO MY COMPANY

- Improved morale

- Decreased time wasted on reactions to my words and tone
- Increase in quality and productivity
- They do not have to continue having conversations with me about this.

BENEFITS TO ME

- I will feel better about myself.
- I will be more likely to receive a promotion.
- I will have more time because there will be fewer complaints.
- I will get a larger bonus because we will be more profitable.

IMPACT FEEDBACK COMPARED WITH AUTHORITATIVE FEEDBACK

DIRECTIVE	IMPACT
"We are up against a deadline. Stop gathering data and summarize conclusions from what you have."	"I am feeling some pressure about our deadline. I think we have spent enough time gathering data and summarizing conclusions." (Commentary: "feeling pressure" and "I think" are impacts.)
"Management has decided to go with plan B. Take care of your assignments now."	"Management has decided to go with plan B. I need assignments completed now." (Commentary: the impact of management's decision is that "I need something," not "you should do something.")

CONTINGENCY	IMPACT
"You missed another deadline. If this continues, I will have no choice but to replace you."	"You missed another deadline. I am concerned." Commentary: no implied threat; hopefully, the receiver will engage about the fact that you are concerned. It can be very effective to use a hybrid Impact and Contingency statement, "I am concerned that this will lead to discipline if it continues."
"If you work on this taskforce, you will get some visibility among senior management."	(Commentary: this is a great example of a case when Impact feedback may be less effective than Contingency. An Impact statement like "I believe you will get some visibility among senior management" probably does not add value. Regardless of the exact words, your tone and body language are most likely to determine how the receiver reacts.)

ATTRIBUTION	IMPACT
"Good job."	"I am delighted by the work done." Commentary: "Good job" labels the receiver's efforts. "I am delighted" reveals the feedback giver's reaction.
"You took your eye off the ball."	"Senior management is thinking you lost your focus." Commentary: this changes the focus from what the feedback receiver did to the Impact on others in the organization.

How To Select An Executive Coach

Imagine you have invested a large portion of your assets in a rapidly growing business with a lot of opportunity—but also many potential threats. Recognizing what is at stake, you decide to retain an executive coach.

What are some of the elements that you need to consider when choosing this person? Which of the following individuals would you hire?

- Someone with an advanced degree in business or psychology who has not owned a business or served as an executive

- Someone with an advanced degree in education who is certi-fied as a master coach and who has not owned a business or served as an executive

- Someone who has no degrees or certifications (perhaps has not finished high school) who has successfully built and sold several similar businesses

- Someone who has extensive experience in senior leadership roles in a corporation much larger than your business, has experience consulting with corporations and large businesses, and has a coach certification

The truth is that selecting an executive coach who is the right fit for you can be a challenge. There is no universally accepted defi-nition of—or standards for—coaching, and there are many models and sub-specialties. The sub-specialties include executive coaching, leadership coaching, career and transition coaching, emotional intel-ligence coaching, business coaching, life coaching, and many others.

In a 2004 *Harvard Business Review* article, "The Wild West of Executive Coaching," Stratford Sherman and Alyssa Freas stated, "No one has yet demonstrated conclusively what makes an executive coach qualified or what makes one approach to executive coaching better than another."

Reviews continue to cite the lack of research on outcome and effectiveness. However, the authors of these reviews generally believe that executive coaching is effective and provides value to the coachees and to their organizations. Other research has similar conclusions.[7] Given the state of the field, I want to provide my perspective on how to select an executive coach. I strongly suggest you seek out other perspectives and do due diligence as you invest in coaching.

COACHING VS. CONSULTING

CAMP 1

Many coaches make a rigid distinction between coaching and consulting. I identify them as Camp 1.

A dominant belief in in this camp is that coaching is about asking powerful questions to help you identify your purpose or *why* and to uncover your own answers and solutions. Coaches in this camp believe that they should not share their knowledge, expertise, and experience. That is for consultants, counselors, mentors and perhaps even therapists to do, but not coaches. In recent years, this group of coaches has become more flexible and will engage in very brief sharing of knowledge and expertise as long as they ask permission.

CAMP 2

Those in this group deeply respect the validity and value of asking powerful questions to help you identify your purpose (your *why*) and to uncover your own answers and solutions. In addition, they

---

7   Diane Coutu and Carol Kauffman, "What Coaches Can Do For You," *Harvard Business Review*, January 2009. https://hbr.org/2009/01/what-can-coaches-do-for-you.

firmly believe that executive coaches add the most value for their clients when they share their knowledge, expertise and experience. This does not mean giving advice or telling you what to do. Most coaches believe that you need to evaluate the input you get and determine whether it is appropriate to act on it in your environment.

I am in the second camp. I do ask permission to share models, process, and techniques. I also make it clear that I am not telling you what to do. I am providing alternative perspectives and information to help you increase your options.

CERTIFICATION/CREDENTIALS

There are numerous professional organizations that provide a certification or credential for coaches and or executive coaches. Among them, in alphabetical order, are the Association of Corporate Executive Coaches, the Center for Credentialing & Education, the International Association of Coaching, the European Mentoring & Coaching Council, the International Coach Federation, and the Worldwide Association of Business Coaches. I am a member and am certified by two of them.

To assist you in making your selection of the best fit, I will describe my perception of the difference between two of the organizations from which I have a coach certification. I will provide a more in depth description of the International Coach Federation because it is the most recognized credential.

THE INTERNATIONAL COACH FEDERATION

The International Coach Federation (ICF) is arguably the largest and most powerful professional coach association in the world (www. coachfederation.org). ICF defines coaching as "partnering with clients in a thought-provoking and creative process that inspires them to maximize their personal and professional potential."

Many corporations, companies, and organizations (such as the United States Federal Government) will engage only coaches who are certified by ICF as a Professional Certified Coach (PCC) or Master Certified Coach (MCC). The criteria for obtaining the MCC credential are 200 hours of coach-specific training, 10 hours of mentor coaching, a minimum of 2,500 hours of coaching experience with at least 35 clients, a performance evaluation of two audio recordings of coaching sessions submitted along with transcriptions, and passing a Coach Knowledge Assessment.

Even though I have executive leadership background and I am a licensed therapist, I received a valuable perspective and training about coaching from an ICF certified training program called the Coaches Training Institute (CTI). I respect this training enough that there are both CTI and ICF certified coaches I would recommend to my family. Personally, I chose to pursue and have become a Professional Certified Coach (PCC).

There are many master level executive coaches who have ICF certification at the PCC or MCC level. However, ICF certification does not require any leadership, business, or organizational background. Nor does it require education in psychology, business, human development, or any other related field.

Over the years, the official ICF position is that coaching is primarily a Camp 1 process though, in my experience, ICF certified coaches may be in Camp 1 or Camp 2. It is hard for me to imagine a successful executive coach who is not in Camp 2.

ICF was originally formed as the professional organization and certifying body for what are today most commonly recognized as life coaches or business coaches. For many years, ICF promulgated only the Camp 1 perspective on coaching. In recent years, ICF has become more flexible about coaches sharing knowledge, expertise, and experience as long as it is with permission and kept to a minimum.

Many executive coaches who are certified by ICF acknowledge that an executive coach must share knowledge and expertise to provide value to the people and organizations they serve. My perspective is that the most successful executive coaches provide a combination of coaching and consulting.

In recent years, an increasing number of executive coaches have become ICF certified for two reasons. The first is that most certified ICF training programs provide a very solid foundation of knowledge, coaching skills, and ethics. This is especially attractive to people with business backgrounds with limited experience in consulting or coaching.

The second reason is to satisfy the market demand for certification. ICF is the most recognized certifying body for coaches, and many companies and organizations throughout the world require ICF certification.

THE ASSOCIATION OF CORPORATE
EXECUTIVE COACHES (ACEC)

The Association of Corporate Executive Coaches (ACEC) is a professional organization that was founded in 2011 to make a "clear distinction between executive coaches whose clients mostly reside in the top third of an organization or government and all other coaches including business coaches." ACEC defines corporate executive coaches as enterprise-wide business partners.

ACEC is associated with the MEECO Leadership Institute, which, among other things, serves as the credentialing body for the Master Corporate Executive Coach Credential (www.meeco-institute. org). MEECO stands for Measuring Excellence in Executive Coaching, Employee Enhancement and Culture in Organizations.

Members join ACEC because they want to be associated and share information with the top executive coaches in the world. All members meet the criteria for and are certified as a Master Corporate Executive Coach (MCEC). The core of the criteria for the MCEC include the following: academic and professional proficiency, 7 to 10 years of experience coaching senior level clients, experience being responsible for the profitability of an organization (other than your own), management of the bottom line, and recognition from professional colleagues. The application process for ACEC requires interviews with client references and colleagues who can attest to the applicant's coaching skill. The applicant is interviewed by a member of the certification committee.

Because ACEC is a relatively young association, the MCEC credential is not yet recognized as widely as the ICF or other credentials.

Therefore, many ACEC coaches have certifications from other organizations as well.

In my experience, the most effective executive coaches provide a mixture of coaching, consulting and mentoring. They do ask powerful questions to help you identify and articulate who you are and what you stand for, your *why*. They also help you uncover your own answers and solutions. In addition, they are willing to share their deep expertise in business, leadership, human development, psychology, etc. When you don't know what you don't know, they are able to teach models, processes, and skills. They do not tell you what to do. They simply provide the information you need to make a more effective decision.

BACKGROUND AND CREDENTIALS

The following are the background and credentials I have used when engaging a coach:

- 5 to 10 years of business or organizational experience and demonstrated success in **"helping executives, leaders, and managers get business results and develop their organizations and themselves"** in the areas relevant to me (or the people who will be coached in my organization.) Minimally, "demonstrated success" means backed up with references and testimonials. Ideally, it means with data measuring the impact of his/her interventions.

- Trust, credibility, and "chemistry" with me or the person being coached.

- Certification and experience with a variety of personality, behavior style and 360-degree assessments (or with those that have already been selected by your organization).

- Can offer business, strategic, organizational, production, and performance management models, processes, and skills that are in alignment with what others or I need.

- Good return on investment.

HIGHLY DESIRED

- Advanced training and/or degree in one of the following disciplines: business; management; leadership; education; training; learning and development; clinical counseling; organizational, educational, or developmental psychology; business process improvement.

  o 5 years' experience with one of the major organizations that provide leadership development and/or executive coaching. Examples are the Center For Creative Leadership, The Blanchard Companies, and Personnel Decisions International.

  o 125 hours of coach specific training up to successful completion of a coach specific training program in which the curriculum is targeted to executive leadership, and management coaching.

DESIRED:

- Independent third-party coach certification

THE SELECTION PROCESS[8]

In selecting an executive coach, I suggest that you get as clear as possible on your goals and outcomes. Are you looking to improve your leadership, business acumen, strategic thinking, interpersonal skills or the ability to manage yourself? What will be different if you achieve your goals?

Then, I recommend asking people you respect and trust for referrals for executive coaches they believe can help you achieve your specific goals and outcomes. As a No-Bullshit Executive, I suggest that you interview these coaches and ask about their background and approach to your goals and outcomes. Here are some key questions to answer for yourself:

1. Are they credible to me?

2. Do I trust them?

3. Do they seem to genuinely want to work with me?

4. Do they have the courage to challenge me directly?

5. Am I comfortable with the confidentiality conditions (limits on confidentiality)?

6. Do they have a defined method for, and demonstrated track record of, working successfully with leaders who are identified as abrasive or bullies?

7. Does the coach conduct initial interviews with my boss, superiors, coworkers and reports to collect detailed

---

8   I want to acknowledge Laura Crawshaw, author of *Taming The Abrasive Manager, How To End Unnecessary Roughness in the Workplace,* for her additions to the key questions in this section.

information on the specific behaviors they identify as problematic? (This is essential to help you develop awareness of, and insight into, how you are experienced by others.)

8. Do they conduct further rounds of coworker interviews as the coaching proceeds to gauge progress, or lack thereof?

9. Does the coach understand that I may be one example of an organizational culture that encourages behavior that would be considered abrasive or bullying?

10. Do I like their approach and process for working with people like me?

11. Do they have additional knowledge and expertise that will add value for me?

12. Is progress measured by ongoing feedback from my coworkers and reports gathered by my employer vs. the coach's opinion and prognosis?

13. Do I believe I will get a good return on investment?

14. Do they have references I can contact?

Selecting a coach is mostly about trust, credibility and chemistry or comfort. I recommend that you interview at least two coaches—if not three or more. You may also want to seek the input of a trusted colleague. In addition to being a sounding board for you, you might ask your colleague to interview the top two coaches as well.

I am a member of and I highly recommend *The Boss Whispering Institute*, which trains coaches in the only defined method to date for coaching abrasive leaders. I encourage you to contact the Institute to locate an executive coach with this exceptional training.

ABOUT THE AUTHORS

Jordan Goldrich

Jordan Goldrich leverages his background as a chief operations officer, professional certified coach, master corporate executive coach, and licensed clinical social worker to partner with senior executives to drive results while developing themselves, their teams, and their organizations. His clients benefit from his ability to help them create direction, alignment, and trust.

His specialty is working with valuable executives who are identified as abrasive or even bullies, helping them to change the unintended impact of their style by taking their warrior spirit to a higher level. His understanding of warriors has been influenced by his work with The Honor Foundation, a nonprofit organization focused on helping Navy SEALs, Green Berets, and our other special forces communities transition to the civilian workforce.

Mr. Goldrich has over 35 years' experience working successfully as a coach, consultant, or advisor with Fortune 500 corporations, closely held and family-owned businesses, and government and nonprofit organizations. His industry experience includes technology, financial services, healthcare, telecommunications, manufacturing, retail, and nonprofit. He is a partner in a multidisciplinary professional consulting firm, CUSTOMatrix, Inc., and leads their executive coaching practice. He has over twelve years' experience as a senior executive coach with the Center for Creative Leadership.

Mr. Goldrich has an MAED (counseling) and a master's in social work. He is a member of the executive committee of the Association of Corporate Executive Coaches (ACEC) and member of the committee for the Master Corporate Executive Coach (MCEC) certification of the MEECO Leadership Institute.

Walter G. Meyer

Walter G. Meyer is the co-author of four nonfiction books, including *The Respectful Leader*, an Amazon best-selling- and Axiom Award–winning business fable. His critically acclaimed, award-winning, and Amazon-best-selling novel *Rounding Third* was published just before the bullying crisis started making the news. He created a presentation, "Accept and Respect: The Keys to Ending Bullying," which he has taken to colleges, high schools, and corporations across the country, including Raytheon, the Equality Professionals Network, Arizona State University, SUNY-Jamestown, and West Virginia University. He has been on numerous radio and television programs, including NPR.

With Doug Peterson, he is the co-author of *Going for the Green:*

Selling in the 21st Century. He has conducted trainings for corporations in leadership, sales, communications, and productivity. He ghostwrote for Michael D. Huggins in *Going Om: A CEO's Journey from a Prison Facility to Spiritual Tranquility*.

Mr. Meyer's articles have appeared in *Kiplinger's Personal Finance*, the *Los Angeles Times*, the *Orange County Register*, and dozens of other magazines and newspapers.

He is the co-author of a widely produced stage play, *GAM3RS*, which has been optioned to be a television series; in addition, several of his screenplays have been optioned to be movies.

Mr. Meyer has a degree from the School of Communications at Penn State.